# Exposure and Risk:
# The Great Coming Church

# Exposure and Risk:
# The Great Coming Church

## A Half Century of Urban Ministry

George E. Todd with Trey Hammond

ISBN-13: 9781470058722
ISBN-10: 1470058723

**Endorsements for *Exposure and Risk: The Great Coming Church***

*The words "church bureaucrat" do not immediately make the heart palpitate. But George Todd has done the near impossible. His riveting account of his life in various religious hierarchies carries the reader all around the world and into one adventure after another. Todd's life demonstrates that church leaders can indeed accomplish significant things, especially for the poor and marginal peoples of the earth. With candor and gentle humor Todd allows us to follow his winding path, including his fruitful partnership with Saul Alinsky and the community organization movement. He puts a human face on what for many people, even church people, has been a faceless edifice. Here is a chunk of American and world history that will edify many readers.*

- Harvey Cox

Rev. Dr. Harvey Cox – Professor, Harvard Divinity School; author of *The Secular City*, *The Future of Faith*, and *When Jesus Came to Harvard: Making Moral Choices Today*

*George Todd is the quintessential connector of people in the ecumenical community. More than any other of his generation, he created during his active years of ecumenical service as the head of World Council of Churches URM (Urban Rural Mission), a worldwide network of social activists. With his enormous capacity to identify and empower potential young talents, he built an incredible global movement of individuals and community organizations, committed, as he himself is, to the struggle for social justice in all the six continents of the world. Of even greater significance, he knew each of the several thousand people in the network by name. That explains why the unique approach to his book is like a "who's who" in the 20th century ecumenical movement. The book is a must read for theologians, social scientists, ecumenists, ecumenical bureaucrats and anyone interested in knowing why despotic leaders in the 70s and 80s considered URM more of a threat to their unjust rule than communism.*

*- Samuel Kobia*

Rev. Dr. Samuel Kobia – Former General Secretary, World Council of Churches; former General Secretary of Kenya's National Council of Churches; former Executive Secretary of WCC's Urban Rural Mission Office

*In the last half of the 20th century, George Todd stood out as an inspiration for urban ministries. Serving as an inner city pastor, working with churches in East Asia to adapt from rural to urban-industrial society, staffing the Presbyterian Church's Urban Ministry desk and the Urban Industrial Mission Office of the World Council of Churches, he developed an enabling style of ministry which found and equipped potential partners from empowerment ministries around the world. He creatively generated the training and financial resources necessary for this effort, with his style of working in the background and maintaining a low profile. Five continents bear the fruits of George Todd's extraordinary ability to sow the seeds of empowerment in the fertile soil of powerless people. This book is the story of that ministry built by George and his tireless partner, Kathleen Franklin Todd.*

*- Philip Newell*

Rev. Philip Newell – Urban pastor; community organizer; former executive for Presbyterian Church (USA) Community Development Office

*This volume is not just a wonderful biography of George and Kathy's life and ministries or a romantic look back at urban ministry during the last 70 years. For folks who are discerning and wrestling with what ministry will look like in the city now and in the future, George and Kathy's stories provides some wonderful insights for the future development of urban ministry within the global community.*

*- Phil Tom*

Rev. Phil Tom – Inner city pastor; former head of the Presbyterian Church (USA) Urban Ministry Office; Director of the Center for Faith-based and Neighborhood Partnerships at the Department of Labor

*George Todd is a man of deep faith, strategic acumen, extraordinary sensitivity to the demand for justice and a passionate belief in everyday people and their capacity for self-government. His impact on the Christian Church and its relationship to the world was broad and deep. He is one of the unsung heroes of the second half of the 20th century. This memoir tells his extraordinary story.*

- Mike Miller

Mike Miller – Founder and Executive Director, Organize Inc., San Francisco; author, *An Organizer's Tale*; former editor, *Social Policy* Magazine

*I have known George Todd for nearly three decades, and this book is true to the person I know. Here you will see and experience someone who has had as his agenda urban ministry and mission throughout his career, which is quite inspiring as he has worked all around the world. I know personally of his particular focus on community organizing, as he has encouraged congregations to form alliances, empower leaders, and hold public and private institutions accountable for improving the conditions of "the least of these." George's ministry has been a ministry of activism that encouraged activism, with the poor and the disinherited children of God always a priority.*

- Fred Davie

Rev. Fred Davie – Vice-President, Union Theological Seminary; former Program Officer for Faith-Based Community Development, Ford Foundation; former New York City Deputy Manhattan Borough President; former staff of New York City Presbytery

# Table of Contents

# Forward

by Trey Hammond

*"Todd is a marvelously passionate person. He is not a*
*religious man, caring as the religious do, only for their*
*own salvation. He is a Christian, a man whose love for*
*the Word of God embraces his affirmation of the lives*
*of others. Todd enjoys the Gospel, and knows the place*
*where the Gospel is to be lived is in the world."*

— WILLIAM STRINGFELLOW, *MY PEOPLE IS THE ENEMY,* 1964

I CONFESS TO having pushed, pulled, and, sometimes, coerced George into writing this memoir of his life, or more accurately, the life he shared with his partner and wife, Kathy. They have been in the forefront of innovative justice ministry of the Presbyterian Church stretching from the 1950s until today. This is more than just the story of their fascinating lives, but a chronicle of urban ministry in Protestantism and ecumenical circles in the second half of the 20th century. They both were shaped by the tumultuous events of their day, but in turn, they helped shape the times in which they lived by their faithful and courageous work.

This account is a counter-narrative to the critical assessment that the Presbyterian Church got too radically involved in the issues of the day in the 1960s and that the church leadership was out of touch with the concerns of rank and file members. In my estimation, the church leadership, with George being a critical part of that cadre, was listening to the movement of God's spirit in the world and the church responded with a faith that involved both "exposure and risk," to use Todd's operative theological perspective. It was their faith in Christ - his incarnation, his teachings, his cross-bearing, and his resurrection - that took them into the world of their day. I, and many others, felt called to serve the Presbyterian Church precisely because of the kind of courageous faith our church lived out in the 1960s.

I am concerned that the Presbyterian Church today has a willed amnesia about those times and seems risk-averse to living out the justice of Christ's reign in the pressing issues of our day. The church, in the words of Bill Stringfellow, is in danger of acting increasingly "religious," concerned with a narrow definition of salvation, and often blind to the social dimensions of God's interest for all of creation. Jesus' first sermon in Luke 4:18-19 connects personal salvation and societal Jubilee. Christ's life is the most vivid demonstration of the just world God intended. I see this book as testimony to that calling.

George is a man with a passionate faith, a vivid memory, and a flair for stories. He is a lover of language, a keen observer of the world, and has a fascination with people and their personal narratives. This memoir is the result of a series of taped interviews conducted with George when I was working in the role of Coordinator for the Office of Urban Ministry of the national office of the Presbyterian Church (USA) in the late 1990s, a position comparable to the one George held in the 1960s. I felt it important to document the urban work of the Presbyterian Church in that era, as it dealt with issues of race, poverty, and justice. I was particularly interested in the creation of a number of crucial justice organizations and the church's role in the evolution of the congregation-based community organizing movement. The retelling of that work is only one chapter of many important roles Kathy and George played with some of the leading edge work of the church around the world. We translated these conversations into the following text. Admittedly, my biases shaped the interviews, but, thankfully, George and Kathy's story emerges in its fullness. Collaborators in this book project are Flo Craft, who did a masterful job in transcribing the tapes to a first manuscript, and Jovan Rossi, who did helpful documentation and helped draft the bibliography.

A fuller rationale for sharing their story comes from the nomination letter I submitted for the John Park Lee Award which the Todd's received from the Presbyterian Health, Education, and Welfare Association of the Presbyterian Church (USA) for lifetime achievement in justice work in 2007. Here is a snapshot of the memoir that follows and a foretaste of their fascinating story:

> In God's providence, these two remarkable people's lives crossed in New York City in the fall of 1952 and they began a partnership that has lasted 53 years. This union has been shaped by the great events in the church and the world in the second half of the 20th century. They in turn worked to see that the arc of history in this time frame bent towards God's justice, as Dr. King wisely articulated. Given their roots, one would expect that they would lead lives deeply immersed in the events of the day. Kathy was raised by missionary parents in Japan and was baptized as an infant by Toyohiko Kagawa, the great prophetic presence among the poor. She came of age as a part of a bi-racial cooperative farm in the Mississippi Delta just before the Civil Rights Movement. George was raised in a pious family and plunged into the complexities of the "world" on the coattails of his newspaper reporter father. He was also shaped by the crucible of World War II and came home with a commitment to justice.
>
> Their marriage was blessed by the great theologian and social critic, Reinhold Niebuhr, who was an influence in both of their lives. They became an integral part of the Group Ministry of the East Harlem Protestant Parish, one of the most innovative urban ministry experiments of the 20th century. The ministry was an effort to respond to the needs of a troubled section of New York City by starting storefront churches and working with the community to improve service and effect public policies. They

worked with their neighbors on issues of housing, public health, education, police corruption, and drug abuse.

From their experience in the parish, George was invited to teach in Taiwan and other Asian seminaries about urban industrial mission and how the church could organize effective, grassroots responses. They returned to the United States in 1963 where George headed the United Presbyterian Church Office for Urban and Industrial Mission. These were the exciting and turbulent sixties, when the Presbyterian Church was in the forefront of the great issues of the day — the civil rights movement, the anti-war movement, cities in crisis, and the emergence of community organizing. George was instrumental in initiating a number of important justice organizations including the National Low Income Housing Coalition, the Interfaith Center for Corporate Responsibility (ICCR), and the Inter-religious Foundation for Community Organization (IFCO). George became good friends with Saul Alinsky and recognized in community organizing an effective way for churches to move past charity to justice work. In those years, Kathy's energies were focused on raising their four sons — John, Peter, Sam, and Adam.

They left New York City for Geneva, Switzerland in 1972, where George directed the World Council of Church's Office for Urban and Industrial Mission. There they continued the work of resourcing and connecting emerging movements aimed at social and economic justice and democratic participation by people left out of power in developing nations in Asia, Latin America and Africa. In Geneva, Kathy worked with the ecumenical Frontier Internship in Mission and the World Student Christian Federation, which provided life changing cross-cultural experiences for young people in their efforts of justice, ecology, human rights, and women's equality.

After a decade with the World Council, they returned to the States, where George took the reins of a progressive, community-oriented foundation, Wieboldt, in Chicago. Kathy lent her skill to the Urban Academy, a training center for urban ministry. The pull to return to New York City was strong, so George accepted the responsibility as the Executive Presbyter of New York City Presbytery in 1986. This allowed him to pursue his commitment to vital urban congregations as places of personal and social transformation. Kathy worked for the National Council of Churches where she led exchanges of American church leaders with counterparts in Russia, Korea and the Philippines. She later worked with programs that helped the church's understanding of the work and mission of the United Nations as a forum for global cooperation.

George retired from the presbytery work after a heart attack slowed him down in 1992. Kathy continued her work with the National Council of Churches as the Director of the International Justice and Human Rights Office until 2002. In their retirement, they have continued to serve the church. As a volunteer, Kathy has also continued her leadership with the World Student Christian Fellowship and the social justice work of The Riverside Church.

If I were going to write a book on their lives I would title it "A View of the World from 21G," which is where they live in the Morningside Gardens, a cooperative on the Upper West Side of Manhattan. Their balcony looks out upon one the world's great cities. From it, you can see the places that have shaped their lives — East Harlem, the Interchurch Center, Union Seminary, and Riverside Church. In any given month, people come from all over the country and the world to visit the Todd's and tell stories and conspire about the world as God intended. Their home is an oasis of hospitality and their care provides strength for others to carry on their work for justice.

One of the correspondences I anticipate every Christmas is the Todd's thoughtful holiday letter, which they have shared with loved ones since their life together began in Harlem. These were *the closing thoughts in their 1990 Christmas letter which probes deeply into the meaning of God's incarnation:*

*"This is the joy and hope of Christmas, that God in person joins humanity as the child of a poor couple. He shatters chaos. He shows in his humility, his healing, his neighborliness, his anger against oppression, his teaching, and his sacrificial living what the human possibilities are. Through this action of God in the life of his people, a way is open to us to join God in overcoming hopelessness and disorder, and in realizing a New World of peace with justice."*

*Kathy remembers that her missionary parents imprinted her with a life-shaping perspective — that every person is born with "an identity, a destiny, and a mission." George and Kathy have very intentionally spent a lifetime following that great calling. The Todd's share with me a love for Shakespeare, and in his play, Twelfth Night, Malvolio says something akin to Kathy's credo. "Some are born great, some achieve greatness, and some have greatness thrust upon them." George and Kathy are humble in the assessment of their lives, all too aware of their flaws, and quite Reformed in their understanding of human nature. But for those of us who have been inspired and nurtured by them, we see in them greatness — that comes from giving one's life to God and others, that is evidenced by an extravagant love that knows no boundaries and by their strong faith that God is still sovereign in a troubled world.*

Bill Stringfellow called his friend George Todd "a Christian" because of his passion for God and humankind and his willingness to live that commitment out wherever God led. George has been blessed to share his life with Kathy, his equal in faith and commitment. They both know the place where the "Gospel is to be lived is in the world" and this world is a better place for their living.

# Preface

by George E. Todd

IT HAS NOT been my ambition to be a writer, but I have taken seriously the requests from people who have encouraged me to set down my recollections for the record. The outcome concerns me because it is supposed to be an account of the trajectory of my life in urban church mission, but having been a church bureaucrat, my focus has in fact instead been primarily on identifying and supporting those people who have been and continue to be engaged in many creative and effective forms of urban church mission throughout the world. I have discovered that institutions in the church bureaucracies where I have worked have been major providers of resources. It has been possible to work with colleagues to direct these strategic resources to projects seeking justice and building communities. Our desire was to support people who were pursuing possibilities for realizing the Biblical vision of the coming kingdom of God, the fulfillment of God's plan for creation.

Nothing has surprised and frustrated me more than to find that after spending ten years in the exciting and challenging ministry of the East Harlem Protestant Parish that I would be spending the next 40 years working in academic and bureaucratic contexts. At the same time, I cannot help but feel satisfaction in having been privileged to have a role over those years in finding ways of bringing the resources of those institutions to support and strengthen dozens of inner city congregations and urban ministries, not only here in the United States but throughout the world, to pursue challenging and sacrificial work on the frontiers of human suffering and need.

I have hoped that I could be telling here the stories of many of the people who have been the heroes, heroines, and carriers of the congregations and programs with which I have been privileged to be involved in encouraging and often finding support for over so many years. In outlining what have become the chapters of this effort, I began by listing some of these important players at each stage of this story. As I did that I found that within a few minutes I had a list of well over fifty names and it has grown exponentially over time. A whole book could be written about the life and work of each one of these named. What I must settle for here is in the way of acknowledgment of some of those with whom I have worked most closely as colleagues and carriers of work described in these pages.

It has been some time since Trey recruited me to work with him in producing this story of how the churches have been responding to the development of cities in the United States and the rest of the world during the second half of the 20th century. He had determined that because of the ways I had been vocationally involved over those years as a pastor in urban congregations and in both denominational and ecumenical efforts to discern the church's response to the city, and that Kathy also had important leadership roles, that this story would be shaped around the events of our life and work. Trey proposed using tapes to work with me on an oral history. I am indebted to him for the ongoing discipline necessary to shape an oral record into eight chapters of this manuscript which I hope will put some coherence to this history of urban church mission covering the past 50 years.

Trey and I met when he visited the World Council of Churches on a trip to East Africa from McCormick Seminary in 1975 and we became friends and colleagues. I have been inspired by his unwavering dedication in exploring what the church is called to be in contemporary cities, as evidenced by his work in Dallas and Albuquerque. His work in community organizing, hunger, affordable housing, public education and justice for people experiencing homelessness has demonstrated how vital local congregations can effect tangible change. I am honored that Trey encouraged me to reflect with him on my own fifty years and more of urban ministry.

When Trey and I began this writing project I told him I wanted to use "Exposure and Risk" as a title. When I look back on what we have done, perhaps the theme, "The Great Coming Church" is more apt. I first heard the expression as a college student in the Student Christian Movement and was challenged with the vision of what the church could be. As I look at what we have written, it seems that I have spent more than 60 years at the task of trying to be a part of bringing that church into being.

At the same time I did not want to abandon the original title. I have been able to see, from day to day and from year to year, people who have taken up the cross, who have made it their life's work to embrace the calling to meet Christ among the poor, the oppressed, the captives, and the blind (Luke 4: 18-19). As what had become my own vocation took me across the USA and around the globe, in hundreds of places I found myself with people who had gone to live and work where they were exposed to pressing human need and whose life often included risk to themselves, their families, their jobs and income and their health. Many of them had no ready or easy promise of success. Yet again and again I have found myself with people who were visibly experiencing the resurrection power which Christ promises to those who walk with him: joy, energy, imagination, hope, and new creation. Halleluia!

## Chapter 1 - Early Life and Education

Saul Alinsky, Margaret Applegarth, Beverly Asbury, Jim Ashbrook, Pat Cober Ashbrook, Ann Austin, Charles Baldwin, Bob and Betty Batchelder, Al Beardslee, Dietrich Bonhoeffer, Martin Buber, William Sloane Coffin, Harvey Cox, John Deschner, Bill and Ann Ellis, Jacques Ellul, Lexie Ferrell, John Fesperman, Sam and Dorothy Franklin, Harry Ford, Bob and Joan Forsberg, Gary Indiana public schools, Dick Gary, Gregor Goethals, Leland Gordon, Barbara Hall, Abraham Heschel, Betty Lou Horton, Betty Johns, Judson Memorial Church, Martin Luther King, Jr., Maggie Kuhn, Peter Lawson, Sue Carpenter Low, Phil Marden, Kenneth Maxwell,

Bill May, Agnes McClain, Jim McGraw, William Lee Miller, Paul Minear, Howard Moody, William Muehl, Ann Austin Murphy, Davie Napier, Reinhold Niebuhr, Richard Niebuhr, Lucy New, D.T. Niles, Garry Oniki, Milan Opecenski, Al Pitcher, Emma Pitcher, Liston Pope, Ed Powers, Metz Rollins, Don Shriver, David Siegenthaler, Sam Slie, Carl Smith, Harry Smith, Luther Smith, Robert and Alice Spike, John Stettner, Masao Takenaka, Molly Seasholes Taylor, Ed Tyler, John Turnbull, Kenneth Underwood, US Army Eighth Armored Division, United Steel Workers of America, Ralph Waite, Bill and Alice Wimer, Dean and Margaret Wright, George and Dodie Younger.

## Chapter 2 - East Harlem Protestant Parish
Helen Archibald, Banks family, Don and Ann Benedict, Flossie Borgman, Jim and Jean Breeden, Coleman Brown, Eugene Callender, George and Buffy Calvert, Al Carmines, Angel Comacho, Wayne Cowan, Colin Connery, Bob and Evelyn Davidson, Norman and Peggy Eddy, Msgr. Jack Egan, Lee Gartrell, Dick Gary, Leola Glover, Kathleen and John Green, Raymond Grist, Marvin Halverson, Archie Hargraves, Chris and Pudge Hartmire, Edler Hawkins, Satoshi Hirata, Hugh and Harriet Hostettler, Laura Jervis, Butch Kelly, Will and Frances Kennedy, Lanoussee family, David Little, Frances Maeda, George McLeod, Jim McGraw, Charles Merrill, Kang Moon Kyu, George Ogle, Sy Ostrow, Ron and Jan Perrin, Jim Robinson, Steve Rose, Letty Russell, Bob Seaver, Diane Schoonover, Dick Shaul, Margaret Shannon, Dick Siciliano, John Coventry Smith, Dick Snyder, Leonard Styche and Annette Ahlman, Mary Lou Taggart, James Tanis, Edna Taylor, Terrell family, Connie Thurber, Ralph Waite, Alice and William Ware, Charles West, Ed and Louise White, Olivia Williams, James Wylie family, and Bill Yolton.

## Chapter 3 - The Taiwan Experience
Boris and Clare Anderson, Chu Kheng Su, Shoki Coe, Peyton and Mary Craighill, Go Ching Khun, Hsiao Ching Fen, Hsiao Tien Kao, James Lee,

Jerome Lee, Richard Lee, Loh Itoh, Peng Ming Men, Song Soan Seng, Te Ji Giok, Don and Marie Wilson, Euton Williams, and Ben Woo.

## Chapter 4 - Urban Industrial Ministry, Presbyterian Church (USA

Thelma Adair, Henry Aguilan, Jae-Woong Ahn, Rubem Alvez, Ann Anderson, Chuho Awe, George and Shirley Bennette, Margaret Bianchi, Don Black, Eugene Carson Blake, Ray Bowden, Fred Bronkema, Barbara Brown, Bob and Sydney Brown, Coleman Brown, Aaron Buell, Kyoji Buma, David Burgess, Feliciano Carino, Ed Chambers, Saral Chatterji, Jose and Eva Chipenda, Chi Song Cho, Sam Clark, Colin Connery, Harvey Cox, Harry and Kieran Daniel, Jairaj and Lakshmi Daniel, Tom and Helga Day, Ned Dewire, Truman Douglas, Jim Drake, Carl Dudley, David Dyson, Msgr. Jack Egan, Dwayne and Kathy Epps, Leon Faniel, Jessica Fernandez, Margaret Flory, Sam Folin, Lyle Franzen, Paulo Freire, Tom Gaudette, Bryant George, Fred Goff, Grace Goodman, Roberto Gonzales, Bill Grace, Douglas Grandgeorge, Lenten and Evelyn Gunn, Anne and Stanley Hallett, Bruce Hanson, Bobbie Wells Hargleroad, Dick Harmon, Beverly Harrison, Jim Harrison, Pharis and Jane Harvey, Mildred Hermann, Chris Iosso, Jesse Jackson, Kim Jefferson, Robert Johnson, Henry Jones, Ken Jones, Park Sang Jung, Arthur Keyes, Yong Bok Kim and Marian Kim, Kabiru Kinyanjui, Bethel Kipligat, June Kushino, Ho Kyun Kwan, Charles Leber, Jr., Charles Leber III, Samuel and Dug Soo Lee, Lorna Lewis, Spence Limbocker, John Lindner, Bryce and Phyllis Little, Dan Little, David Little, Bob Lodwick, Frances Maeda, Harry Mahakian, Bong Malanzo, Lloyd and Alice Marcus, Francois Mbea, Joyce Manson, Phil Marden, Scott Matheny, Vern McCarty, Jim McDaniel, Joe Merchant, Mike Miller, Steven Moon, Richard Moore, James Morton, John Moyer, John Oliver Nelson, Philip Newell, Randy Nugent, Tony Nugent, Kenneth Neigh, Milton Nunez-Coba, Ron O'Grady, Jae Shik and Ock Shin Oh, Jim Palm, Ming Pan, Hyung Kyu Park, Mary Jane Patterson, Ruth Prudente, Manuel Quintero, David and Betty Ramage, Jovelino Ramos, Jon Regier, Syngman Rhee, Benton and Doris Caldwell

Rhoades, Negail Riley, Alphonso Roman, Roy Romer, Dan Rose, Betty Rosenbloom, Eunice Santana, John Scotland, Marshall Scott, Jim Sessions, Rajan Singh, Richard Snyder, Hans and Ellie Spiegel, Susan Stack, Peg and Les Stansbery, Diana Stephen, Ray Swartzback, Bert Tom, Phil Tom, Madelaine Tramm, Joel Underwood, John Wagner, Lucius Walker, Jim Wallis, Ed Ward, Monte Wasch, Kenneth Waterman, David Watermulder, Sheldon Waters, Bill Weisenbach, Cornell West, Peter Weiden, Marcel Welty, Frank White, Herbert White, Hugh White, Margaret White, Josef Widjanatja, Gay Wilmore, William Wipfler, Jack Woodard, Charles Yerkes, Francis Yip, Philip and Betty Jean Young, and David Zuverink.

## Chapter 5 - World Council of Churches

Jeffrey and Annathai Abeysekera, Henry Aguilan, Wesley Ariarajah, Brigalia Bam, Canaan Banana, Nita Barrow, Charles Henry Bazoche, Subir Biswas, Fred and Marguerite Bronkema, David Calvert, Burgess Carr, Emilio Castro, Cho Chi Song, Lynn Tate-Clark, Harry Daniel, Edicio de la Torre, Jose DeLuca, Ed File, Raymond Fung, Ted Gill, Alberto Gonzales, Bill Grace, Rosemary Green, Todd Greentree, Trey Hammond, Gerhard Hoffmann, Leon Howell, Ann-Marie Kappeli, Rosemary Kilchenman, Norbert Kline, Samuel Kobia, Paul Loeffler, Raoul Macin, Rabail Mallick, LaVerne and Nellie Mercado, Bill Murrah, Soritua Nababan, John Nakajima, George Ninan, Yushi Nomura, Bill Nottingham, Kenichi Otsu, John Poor, Philip Potter, Ruth Prudente, Konrad Raiser, Dawn Ross, W.J. Rumambi, Carlos Sabanes, Eunice Santana, Horst Simanofsky, Krista Springe, Ruth and Arnie Sovik, General Simatupang, Koson Srisang, Kim Kwan Suk, Toshiri Takami, Betty Thompson, John Thurber, Machteld von Vredenbergh, Thomas Wieser, Marcus Woo, Ted Wickham, and Ursula Zierl.

## Chapter 6 - Wieboldt Foundation

Onnie Darrow, Diane Glenn, Robert Matthews Johnson, Craig Kennedy, Lawrence Kennon, Jeff Krehbiel, Lance Lindbloom, John McKnight, Garry

Oniki, Shep Parsons, Dick Poethig, Rita Simo, Dick Simpson, and Art Smith.

## Chapter 7- New York City Presbytery

Paule Alexander, Bob Brashear, Richard Butler, Effie Bynum, David Cockcroft, Bob Davidson, Fred Davie, David Dyson, Cornell Edmonds, Shirley Fleming, Mike Gegan, Adolfo Griffith, James Harrison, Alice Hudson, Laura Jervis, Chris Kim, Lou Knowles, Bryant Kirkland, Kosuke Koyama, Florence Kraft, Pat Laws, Moon He Lee, Lorna Logan, Jim and Mary Martin, Bob McClendon, Mildred McGee, Mary McNamara, Millie Mead, Steven Moon, Paul Moore, Alicia Nebot, Patrick O'Conner, Herbert Oliver, Nicholas Otieno, Annie Rawlings, David H. C. Read, Vera Roberts, Margaret Scott, Gil and Cecilia Sherman, Jim and Laurie Speer, Melanie Squillante, and Ben Zion.

Again, this list should be so much longer. Kathy and I feel surrounded by this great cloud of witnesses whose example and whose care for us continues to inspire and support us in these days of our retirement.

# CHAPTER 1

—— ❧ ——

# Coming of Age: Born into the Tumultuous 20th Century (1925-1951)

THE TWENTIETH CENTURY, for the United States of America and the rest of the world, was a time of unprecedented change and ferment. This era included two world wars, severe economic depressions, urbanization, the end of the colonial era with liberation movements and new nations emerging, the Cold War, the nuclear age, technologies transforming communication and transportation, emergence of a global economy, women struggling for and gaining rights, civil and human rights campaigns for many peoples, ecological consciousness, and many other great movements.

Dietrich Bonhoeffer, the German theologian and martyr, reflecting on this era while in a Nazi prison, called the 20th century "The World Come of Age." In *Letters and Papers from Prison*, he called for the church to be engaged with people and the world around us in ways that are commensurate with all its challenge, beauty, and complexity. He described that engagement as "religionless Christianity" and becoming "a church existing for others." He condemned contemporary Protestant churches for being too absorbed in their own internal affairs and idolaters of their own history, doctrine, and priorities.

For most of my adult life, my work has been centered in the life of the church. I am grateful for having been called into ordained ministry. Reflecting on my life since my ordination in 1950, I feel blessed to have been placed among colleagues and fellow Christians who were rich with a zest for life, intelligence, imagination, capacity, and talent for love all along the road. I have been surrounded by so great a cloud of witnesses who have been struggling to realize the coming into being of a church fulfilling the possibilities and aspirations of its biblical founders and of prophets, martyrs, apostles, ministers, missionaries, and the committed baptized members of innumerable congregations of people who are carriers of the vision, hope, and expectations which Christians such as Bonhoeffer foretold.

My twin brother, Rowland, and I were born in Walworth County Hospital in Lake Geneva, Wisconsin, on June 7, 1925. The hospital at that time also served as a shelter for homeless and needy people of that small community. My family liked to recall that the twins had been born in "the poor house." My father, Arthur, owned a print shop and was also the editor and publisher of the Lake Geneva weekly newspaper, which announced our birth with a banner headline. The Todd's came from Scottish and English roots. Christopher Todd was the first of our American family line arriving in 1622, the year after the Mayflower had landed. The second pilgrim's ship carried in it craftspeople, like my forebear who was a carpenter, because the first wave of Puritans was strong in faith, but short on farming and building skills in facing their first harsh winter.

My maternal grandfather, George Sheets, came from German Protestant stock. His family had immigrated to western Pennsylvania in the early 19th century, where he settled among the Pennsylvania Deutsch. He graduated from Colgate-Rochester Divinity School in Rochester, New York, where he studied with Walter Rauschenbusch, a pioneer of Social Gospel theology. While in Rochester, he met and married Ida Young, personal secretary to the president of the Waterman Pen Company. Rev. Sheets became a prominent American Baptist minister serving several congregations in Illinois. He was active in the Northern Baptist denomination and theological education.

While he was the pastor of the First Baptist Church in Rockford, Illinois, his daughter Grace, a recent graduate of Rockford College, worked as a school teacher. She met my father, a young reporter for the *Rockford Star*, in the church's young adult group. They married in 1924 and soon moved to Lake Geneva, Wisconsin, where he edited the local paper.

When my sister Pat came along in 1927, my parents concluded that they could not support a growing family by running a small newspaper and print shop. We moved to Youngstown, Ohio, a big steel mill town, where he became a reporter with a larger paper, the *Youngstown Telegram.* Shortly after we moved, my sister Doris was born in 1929.

We were all actively involved in the First Baptist Church of Youngstown, where all four of us kids went to Sunday School. My father became Sunday School superintendent. From the great semi-circle of fixed pews in the sanctuary, where my family regularly filled a whole row, we faced a floor to ceiling mural showing the angels announcing the birth of Christ to the shepherds. Faith was central in my parents' lives and being a part of the church in our growing up years significantly shaped the persons we were becoming. When my brother and I were twelve years old, we responded to the altar call, confessing our faith. At Easter time, we were baptized by immersion, both of us in one dip on the minister's arm.

As a child it was still an exciting event whenever an airplane flew overhead. We'd all run outside and look up to see it. We children would gather around the radio, a "modern invention," after school to listen to "Buck Rogers in the Twenty-first Century," "Jack Armstrong, the All-American Boy," and "Little Orphan Annie." Television was still many years away.

Music was an important part of my growing up. We had a piano and my parents would often sing with the kids at bedtime. We learned hymns, spirituals, folk songs, and popular music. "Mae D. Scott, Teacher of Piano" was the little sign on the instructor's clapboard house where my brother and I took weekly piano lessons for five years. I played in piano recitals and worked my way up to Debussy's *Claire de Lune.* The lessons ended, but I continued to develop my piano skills, and often played for Sunday School and Wednesday night prayer meeting. Having the ability to get people singing, both popular music and sacred music, has brought me much pleasure over my lifetime. I also played the tuba in the school marching band. My parents were committed to exposing us to great music and secured tickets to local performances of artists like Jascha Heifetz, Paul Robeson, and traveling symphony orchestras.

In the early thirties, as the Depression deepened, many newspapers were forced to merge. *The Youngstown Vindicator* bought the *Telegram*, where my father had become the star reporter. My father was let go when the merged paper decided it could not afford two star reporters. He was recruited by the Republican National Committee as a speechwriter for Alf Landon, who unsuccessfully ran against Franklin D. Roosevelt for president in 1935. After the campaign, with the connections that job afforded, doors opened for my father to get back into reporting, first with the *Indianapolis Star* and later with the *Gary Post-Tribune*. He worked for the Gary paper for more than thirty years, reporting the city beat, until he retired.

At the *Post-Tribune*, he covered local politics – city hall, the school board, the local steel mill and labor unions, and crime, police, and the courts. Sometimes after church on Sunday, my father took my brother and me along when he interviewed prisoners in the city jail while working on a story. We never forgot the locking, unlocking, and clanging of doors in the prison. There were times when my father was covering controversial stories that rocks were thrown through the window of our home. Sometimes my Dad would take my brother and me when he was covering a crime scene. My first job was being hired by my father as a runner to carry his notes from a trial at the courthouse to the newspaper in time for deadlines.

My father's skill as a reporter was never more evident than when shortly before his retirement in 1970 he was assigned to edit a series of special editions of the newspaper, in observance of the 50th anniversary of the founding of Gary, chronicling the city's history. Special issues were produced on the growth of the steel industry, the rise of unions, the development of the school system, Gary's emerging multi-ethnicity, and other facets of city life. That series remains a classic resource for people researching the history of Gary.

I attended the Lew Wallace High School, named for the Indiana author who penned *Ben Hur*. In those days, public schools in Gary were entirely segregated. There were five high schools in town and only one served the African-American community. We lived in a middle-income, all white neighborhood. I was active in music, drama, Student Council, and other typical activities of high school. When my parents learned I had enough credits to graduate after only three years, they thought it would be advantageous for me to start working to save money for college. The United States had just entered World War II and, with the large numbers of young men enlisting and being drafted, the steel mills were looking for manpower. A high school aged kid could make good money, $5-6 per hour, working in the mill. With some reluctance, I graduated early and went to work in the factory in 1942.

My first job was reading the meters in tunnels underneath the ovens converting coal to coke for the smelting operations. Later, I had the job of catching the hot steel with tongs as it flowed from the open hearths into molds that cooled into metal sheets and rods to be used for manufacturing cars. The work was strenuous and dangerous. My hands still have scars from being splashed by molten steel. I joined the United Steel Workers of America, one of the largest and best organized unions at the time, and even put my tuba to work in the union band.

My family was somewhat conservative politically, with my father being a staunch Republican all his life. He had written speeches for Alf Landon, making fun of Roosevelt, and sent home campaign buttons for us kids like "We Don't Want Eleanor Either." My father was understandably upset when he discovered that I had attended a Communist Party meeting with other factory workers. He was anxious to know if I had signed anything at the meeting, but I had not. That was as close as I ever came to the Communist Party as a participant, although I had plenty of exposure to communism in international work later in life.

A few days after my 18th birthday in 1943, my draft notice arrived. Within a few weeks my brother Rowland and I were called up. We went off to basic training together at Fort Benning, Georgia. In the midst of the rigor of boot camp, I was recruited to play the piano for the company jazz band. That gig got me out of the rock-crushing detail that was assigned to my company. Close living with fellow soldiers from across the country, strict military discipline, and a strenuous physical regimen became my way of life for the next four years.

After basic training, my brother and I were selected for assignment to an Army Special Training Program (ASTP). This program was intended to prepare some draftees to become officers. We were sent to the University of Illinois in Champaign where we lived in vacated fraternity houses and took courses in engineering, math and physics. Along with studies, we observed military disciplines of daily calisthenics, drill, and inspection. We had been active for only a short while when one morning, at 6 a.m. inspection, it was announced that we should go back to our rooms, pack our duffle bags, and be prepared to leave later that day for Camp Polk, Louisiana, where we would become part of the Eighth Armored Infantry Division. The invasion of Europe had started and long-term officer training was no longer a priority as troops were needed immediately to carry the invasion forward.

I became a jeep driver in the Eighth Armored Division, even though I did not even have a license to drive a car before entering the Army. It is still a puzzle how I ended up as a driver. I learned how to operate trucks, half-tracks, and tanks. In addition to learning to handle rifles, which we had learned to break down and reassemble in the dark, we were trained to use bazookas, machine guns, and anti-aircraft weapons. This earned Rowland and me ribbons signifying skills as sharpshooters and experts.

By fall, we were transferred to Camp Kilmer, New Jersey, for deployment overseas. We got weekend passes to New York City and would be dropped off in Times Square, like thousands of other wide-eyed soldiers new to the big city. The USO offered free tickets to *Oklahoma* and other Broadway shows that were currently running. It was my first exposure to the excitement of New York.

We were soon loaded onto a ship bound for the European front. While our company was stationed in England, a huge crate arrived for me. It was a jeep with all of its pieces stored in grease. My job was to unpack the box and assemble the vehicle. With help from mechanics in the motor pool, I got the jeep running and was soon driving it, with much slipping and sliding, up the frozen gangplank of a ship in Southampton, bound for Calais, France.

My unit was in combat almost every day from the late fall of 1944 until Victory in Europe Day on May 5, 1945. The Allied forces were pushing the Germans back with intense fighting and shelling. The Eighth Armored Division advanced across eastern France, into Belgium and the Netherlands, and back down into Germany across pontoon bridges and through bombed-out Aachen to the Black Forest where we were posted when the war in Europe ended.

These were an adventurous few months of combat. Some nights we would be housed in the comfort of a big chateau and offered schnapps by the local farmers. Other nights we'd be digging foxholes and shivering in the icy ground. Men were getting killed around me, shells were bursting overhead, and airplanes strafed our vehicles, sending us scrambling into ditches for cover. When a village was taken, one of my company's tasks was conducting house-to-house searches for remaining German troops. Soldiers hiding in coal bins and in attics were rounded up for POW camps. Sometimes in such sweeps, our GIs were rough on the owners of the houses that sheltered German soldiers. War is chaotic and frightening to combatants and civilians alike.

This time of combat, and its intensity, was instrumental in my coming of age. First, war forged close bonds with my company companions. A celebrated experience of the citizen army is that it throws together people from all social classes, educational levels, and different parts of the country. That was certainly true in our company and the friendships cemented in combat, among a disparate bunch of men, lasted a lifetime.

Secondly, it was impossible to ignore the sad plight of refugees. Everywhere people were fleeing the battle with their belongings in wheelbarrows, horses and wagons, and cars of every description. Sometimes the roads were so clogged with refugees that it was hard for military convoys to pass. It was heartbreaking to see all these suffering people, driven from their homes, with the little they could salvage, and unsure where they were going or what the future held.

In our tour of duty, we unsuspectingly came upon a town in Germany which harbored a concentration camp. "Liberating" it was like entering a nightmare. We discovered cadaver-like figures lying on mats in the barracks, some alive and many dead. Surrounding us were gaunt men and women wandering aimlessly through the camp in their striped prison clothes. We made the chilling discovery of open pits of corpses, white with lime, and others full of smoldering ashes where bodies had only recently been cremated. A film of my company's encounter with that camp is part of the exhibition at the National Holocaust Museum in Washington D.C.

Many years after the war I was asked to describe this experience to a group which included a rabbi. He had never met anyone with the first-hand experience of seeing a concentration camp and he asked me a searing question, "How could you do anything else with your life than be a witness to what you saw?"

Immediately after VE Day, a two and half ton truck load of our company were given passes for a quick trip to Paris, making our way through crowds celebrating the end of the war. The next week, some of us got passes for a week-long train trip to Rome, where we saw ancient sites, viewed Mussolini's ubiquitous fascist monuments, and even had an audience with the Pope.

After the end of the war, our company was moved to the Sudetenland in Czechoslovakia, the first piece of land annexed by Germany. Our assignment had us go from house to house, ousting German families, many of whom had been living there for two or three generations, and compelling their return to Germany on a few hours' notice. Our next assignment was working as guards at a large prisoner of war camp from which German soldiers, after screening, were returned to their homes.

Our company was housed with Czech families. A buddy and I were housed at a working farm, which had two young men about our age. We all shared the same room. After months of army rations eaten on the run, eating home-cooked meals every night was a luxury. Our hosts immersed us in Czech culture, taking us to weekly polka dances at the village community hall, seasonal festivals with parades of costumed young people and decorated carts and oxen. We attended operas by Smetana and Dvorak, at the re-opened Pilsen Opera House. On the way to the opera one evening, I was approached by a beautiful woman who turned out to be a Czech movie actress. She asked me if I would marry her, so that she could make her way to America. It was not to be.

After leaving Czechoslovakia, we went back to Bavaria and were stationed in Regensburg, halfway between Munich and Nuremburg. American universities were beginning to prepare for the impact of the newly passed GI Bill which could bring a huge influx of combat veterans into American colleges after the war. As the war wound down, some professors patriotically volunteered to come and teach GI's in Europe, trying to get some feel for how returning vets might fit into their schools. When the notices about these trial American university courses went up, several of us applied and were accepted.

In September 1945, we were shipped off to England for the first term of Shrivenham American University. Classes were offered by such distinguished professors as Charles Hendel, head of the Philosophy Department at Yale University, and the brilliant composer, Benjamin Britten. Weekends were free and we were given British travel vouchers good for all of England and Scotland. We traveled to many of the famous cathedral cities and took advantage of London's art and culture. The Old Vic Theater had re-opened and they had a repertory season that fall of *Oedipus Rex, The School for Scandal,* and *Henry IV - Parts 1 & 2*, with Laurence Olivier playing in all four. Shrivenham was close to Oxford and within walking distance of Stonehenge. I sang in the school choir, which performed at Westminster Abbey in an observance of the American Thanksgiving.

After the semester in England, I returned to Regensberg, Germany as a part of the occupation forces, until being released from the Army in the summer of 1946, leaving with the rank of corporal. We embarked for the States by ship. The sight of the Statue of Liberty in New York harbor brought a cheer from the troops. Welcome delegations met us at the docks and we were home. After my final discharge, a bus pass got me back home to Gary, my family, and my old job at the steel mill.

The next semester, I enrolled at Denison, a Christian liberal arts college in Granville, Ohio, along with my brother, who had been discharged earlier. Many of the students at the school were of Northern Baptist background (my mother's brother, a World War I veteran and the son of a Baptist minister, had been a professor of mathematics at Denison). Religion was an important part of the life of the school. Al Pitcher, the chair of the religion department, taught a course on different approaches to reality. We read four books: *What Is Truth?* by John Dewey, the pragmatist educator and philosopher who taught that truth is what can be observed and measured; *What Is Life?* by Erwin Schroedinger, a Nobel laureate physicist known for his work on wave mechanics and pioneering in RNA research, as he came at life from the standpoint of physics and biology; *Out of My Life and Thought,* by Albert Schweitzer, the musician, theologian, and missionary doctor who viewed life as an expression of God's creation and urged a mystical reverence for all living things; and *Reveille for Radicals* by Saul Alinsky, community organizer, who framed life as a political struggle to acquire, hold, and use power.

While in college, I attended the First Baptist Church in Granville, where Kenneth Maxwell was the minister. He was a remarkable preacher and a model of a "liberal pastor" schooled in the Social Gospel. A graduate of Colgate-Rochester Divinity School, his sermons were stirring, often centered on social issues and current political events. He invited me to be a leader with the church's student programs and soon I was leading the music in church activities. This began my ongoing experience in leading community singing.

Through the church I got involved in national Baptist happenings and became the president of the national association of Baptist students. This opened the door into the World Student Christian Federation (WSCF). Founded in 1890, the WSCF is an international organization of Christian students in countries across the world committed to building community and learning together in universities and other educational settings.

Dean Wright, the Baptist Ohio state staff person for campus ministry, invited me to accompany him to a week-long convocation at Yale Divinity

School. Famous preachers and scholars from all around the world came to give the Beecher lectures on preaching, the Taylor lectures on theology, and others. What I experienced there moved me profoundly. I was going through a time of personal searching. My questions were: "What is life all about? Is there such a thing as value? What is life worth? Does it have any worth at all? Does it matter? Why is one thing better than something else? Why does it matter whether people suffer or die?" These questions were understandable after seeing so many people suffer and die in the war. I thought, "I could be dead, men next to me perished, but I survived. What am I supposed to be doing with my life?" Many of those returning from the war felt the same way.

That there were schools where they addressed such questions as the nature of existence and the meaning of life so seriously was beyond my experience. To be in the midst of that exploration might help with my own questions. Back at Denison, Dr. Pitcher, said, "Maybe you belong at Yale, instead of here. Let's figure out a way for you to go there now." The administration worked with me, finding creative ways to give credits for life experience and special projects and making it possible for me to graduate in 1948, instead of 1950.

I enrolled at Yale Divinity School that fall, not with the intent of studying for the ministry, but to grapple with questions of meaning. Yale had an outstanding faculty to encourage such inquiry: Richard Niebuhr in theology and ethics; Roland Bainton in Christian history; Robert Calhoun and Julian Hart in philosophical theology; and Liston Pope in social ethics. These were giants in the land.

I went as a U.S. delegate to the Central Committee of the World Student Christian Federation Committee meeting in Canada in 1949. We met with leading ecumenical figures like Philip Potter, D.T. Niles, John Deschner, and M. M. Thomas. At those gatherings there was much discussion of the state of the church, what were its current limitations, and what might be done to bring about "the Great Coming Church."

At the same time that I entered Yale, two of my mentors from Denison, Robert Spike and Dean Wright, migrated to New York City for doctoral studies at Columbia. I used to travel from New Haven often to visit. One day they telephoned me at Yale excited that they just might have found the site for "The Great Coming Church!" They took me to Greenwich Village where on Washington Square they pointed to an intriguing structure, the Judson Memorial Baptist Church. It had been built as a memorial to the first Baptist missionary to Burma, the famous Adoniram Judson. We began to scheme about how this place could be a part of this new thing God was doing.

We discovered that the building was rented to New York University for classroom space and offices. The historic congregation had dwindled to about fifteen people who worshiped on Sundays, led by Dan Novotny, a student pastor from Union Seminary. Spike and Wright arranged that I could succeed him when he graduated in June. I came to New York for the summer. We persuaded the Baptist City Society to allow us to attempt to revitalize the congregation and connect with the community. Greenwich Village was known as a center for practicing artists and writers. The community also included a working class neighborhood called Little Italy. The church building itself was surrounded by New York University. Dean and Bob and their wives moved into the building and Dean started serving as a campus minister at NYU. The experiment was off the ground.

The first order of business was to understand and engage the community. There were many gangs in Little Italy and we started programs with the young men and women we met. We supported working families in the neighborhood as they dealt with landlords, police, and local schools. Soon, a vigorous student program built around the tenement, which was part of the church building. The students named it "Happy House" and painted marvelous murals on the walls of the four flights of stairs.

The Judson Dance Theater opened and reached out to the artistic community. Another part of the church opened up as a gallery where artists from the community were welcome to display their art. Renowned artists like Robert Rauschenberg and Robert Indiana exhibited their work at Judson Gallery. The Poet's Theater opened and Judson became a very lively center for the range of performing arts in the community.

Al Carmines graduated from Union in 1958 and came to Judson as co-minister with Bob Spike. Al was a phenomenal musician and composer. He came as close to Bach's "minister of music" role as anybody in the church in modern times. He composed three or four oratorios and cantatas a year, as well as hymns that were sung by the congregation. His oratorios and cantatas were critically acclaimed by art critics and their debuts were much anticipated. He soon built a choir that included professional singers interested in such vital sacred music.

As the vitality and diversity of the community were embraced by the church, Judson congregation flourished in numbers and purpose. In a few years, the leasing of the building to NYU phased out and the building was completely used for ministry. Judson Memorial Church became a model of witness to the city, and still is. Judson Church archives are to be found in the nearby New York University Library building.

In returning to Yale at the end of that first summer as a student pastor, I sensed that becoming a minister was both what I wanted to do and what I was being called to do. My first year of divinity school had helped me start to answer those great burning questions. My own formation for work as a pastor would shape my second and third years of theological study. The faculty at Yale made theology lively. Richard Niebuhr turned every class into an epiphany. His basic framework was an ethic of response. He'd ask, "Right here, right now, what makes this building stand? What's holding the floor up? Keeping your heart beating? So, breathe deeply; this is God creating." We were encouraged to see that through the Bible, and also in the events of the day, that God is present and at work. We were challenged to think ethically and to shape our actions, our responses, and our very lives to God's immediacy.

Kenneth Underwood and Liston Pope gave us skills of correlation, relating Biblical faith and theology to what was transpiring in the life of the world. Underwood taught courses known as the "and" classes: *Faith and Politics*, *Church and the Press*, *Faith and Economic Life*, and *Church and Race*. Professors like Davie Napier and Paul Minear opened the Bible in such a way that it was a living document defining and nourishing who we were as a family of faith.

Some years later I distilled my theological formation at Yale this way:

"Reinhold Niebuhr gave theological students practice in the political skills of discerning the signs of the times, along with the strongest resistance to absolutizing any party, ideology, or strategy within history. Richard Niebuhr taught an ethics of response, equipping Christians to define their vocations in response to a God who is revealed in every event as Creator, Sustainer, Governor, Judge, and Redeemer. Nicolas Berdyaev deepened the sense of a God involved with creation, struggling and groaning in nature and in history to bring that creation into the fullness of God's intentions for its being. Paul Tillich attacked the Protestants' own churches which had become captive to class and nation. He nurtured sensitivity to a Holy Spirit alive in autonomous culture and in history creating new forms of the church for the future. Dietrich Bonhoeffer held up a vision of the possibilities of community in his *Life Together*, and the demands of risk- taking in his development of the theme of "life for others" and "the church for others." Jacques Ellul, in *The Presence of the Kingdom*, held together the absolute character of the Barthian transcendent Word of God over against the world, with the excitement and the mystery of that Word precisely present and powerful in the midst of human events. Helmut Gollwitzer, coming from prison camps, was making Marxist tools available to Christians as a gift of God for realizing fuller justice within the political and economic structures."

Another aspect of the Yale experience was built upon my growing up as the son of a newspaperman. As a student fieldwork assignment, I was hired by the National Council of Churches' communications office to staff a local radio station for religious programming, which mostly involved recruiting church choirs and guest preachers. Thinking about that job with the tools of "correlation" articulated in classes like *Church and the Press*, led me to explore how "religious radio" could be about more than choirs and preachers. Barth famously spoke of "reading the Bible in one hand and a newspaper in the other." A group of eight or ten students met every Wednesday to explore key headlines and discuss the news stories from a religious and biblical perspective. The group included many extraordinary folks who went on to significant careers in the church and academia, such as William F. May, Ann Austin, Bob Lynn, William Lee Miller, David Graybeal, John Turnbull, and Dick Gary.

Theologically, we built upon Richard Niebuhr's perspective that God related to creation through five kinds of actions - creating, sustaining, governing, judging, and redeeming. If one embraces such a conviction, one can explore how these divine activities are concretely taking place. Could the ways God was relating to creation be seen in the stories we are reading in the newspaper? Could such analysis provide the basis for a weekly broadcast trying to look at the news "from God's perspective?"

This led to "Religion at the News Desk," a weekly broadcast offering theological exploration and commentary on the events of the day. On Wednesdays, our group would get together and look at the newspapers. Could we discern God's presence in the baseball World Series? Was it in the crossing of the 38th parallel in Korea? We'd assign unfolding events to individuals for research and analysis. Bill Miller and I would pull the briefs together, write a script, and read it live over air on Saturday evening at 6:00 PM. Our professors - Richard Niebuhr, Bill Muehl, and Kenneth Underwood - would listen to and critique the broadcasts. "Religion at the News Desk" lasted for another ten years or so and remains a part of the mythos of Yale Divinity School.

Even today, an aspect of my devotional life is daily reading the New York Times and other papers, with an eye to see how each story reveals something about the way that God is working in history and in individual lives, as well as ways in which we human beings thwart God's intentions. Correlating the world's news and the Good News makes for a rich morning spiritual practice. Where can we glimpse God's engagement with the world and what might God be asking of me and of the human family? Which news stories called for praise and thanksgiving, for intercession, for confession, and for offering commitments and actions?

As I graduated, I was ready to leave seminary and begin my career in the church. The idea of "the great coming church" and my experience at Judson and the Student Christian Movement attracted me to new experiments in ministry, rather than seeking a job in an established congregation.

My experience in the steel mills and in the war, followed by this time of biblical and theological reflection, had begun to lead me toward two life convictions - exposure and risk. Christian life is a call to exposure to what is going on in the world at places of suffering, struggle, and injustice. Exposure leads to a life of risk. To enter into solidarity with those in difficult circumstances means undertaking tasks and actions where one cannot know the outcomes. Such risk is what Christ meant when he invited us "to take up the cross and follow me," knowing it might lead us to a kind of crucifixion. Resurrection and the inflowing of Christ's life-giving spirit come as such choices are made.

Nothing seemed like a more challenging place to begin ministry than an experiment just underway in New York City called the East Harlem Protestant Parish. I was familiar with some of the key leaders in the movement. I became convinced that in joining them I was following a call to where God was leading. I left New Haven for New York City and East Harlem in June of 1951.

# CHAPTER 2

— ❧ —

# A Ministry Different: The East Harlem Protestant Parish (1951-1959)

THE EAST HARLEM Protestant Parish was one of a number of experimental ministries in the United States and Europe that emerged in the post-World War II years. These efforts explored new forms of Christian community in response to the "world coming of age" that Bonhoeffer articulated from prison. These movements, emerging in a number of places where traditional Western ecclesial structures were strong, shared in common an openness to how God might be calling people into the pressing needs of the day with new ways of communal Christian life.

During the decade that I was living and working in East Harlem, the World Student Christian Federation was completing an extended Biblical and theological study on the life and mission of the church. Following that WSCF study, the World Council of Churches carried on a decade-long exploration pursued by study groups in each of its five regions called *The Missionary Structure of the Congregation*. A number of books and reports emerged in the course of this study. Some of the publications came out of the study itself while others came out of local and regional experiments searching for new shapes for the church in the mid- and late 20th century. One expression which became widely used during that time was "morphological fundamentalism." Alongside the familiar discussions about Biblical fundamentalism came a critical look at a kind of fundamentalism seen as a rigid and inflexible attitude toward existing forms of Christian community taken to be fixed once and for all, rather than systems emerging during periods of church history specific to the needs of those times. Were there other forms of Christian community besides the traditional congregation that were coming into being? Some of the key leaders in these discussions were Thomas Wieser, Colin Williams, Hans Hoekendijk, Bill Webber, Paul Loffler, Jitsuo Morikawa, D.T. Niles, M.M. Thomas, Werner Simpfendorfer, Christa Springe, Hugh White, Robert Spike, and Letty Russell.

In Scotland, a group of clergy and laypeople, feeling a call for the church to build vital ministries in low income and working class communities in Glasgow, sought inspiration from the example of St. Columba. This exiled Irish saint, in the 6th century, used the island of Iona as a base to share and live the faith among the Celtic people of Scotland. In the 1930s, under the leadership of George McLeod, a visionary Church of Scotland pastor, urban leaders gathered on Iona for prayer and reflection. They committed themselves to restore the chapel and other monastic buildings and create an Iona Community open to new expressions of music, liturgy, and ministry. The Iona Community explored ways that members could give mutual support in shaping their individual, family and vocational lives, as well as working for significant ministry in inner city Glasgow. They committed to one another to follow "a rule of life", with disciplines defining their use of money, their use of time, their spiritual practices of prayer and study, and their work for social justice.

In England, the *Industrial Mission* movement was underway as the Bishop of Sheffield, Ted Wickham, explored the possibility of congregations drawn from vocational affiliations as well as from geographical parishes. Some pastors met with people in their workplace for prayer, discussions of work-related issues and personal concerns. Other pastors took jobs working in the factories and sought ways of ministering among their co-workers.

In France, there were a number of movements in the Catholic community - the Mission Populaire, the Worker Priests, and the Young Workers Movement. The book, *France: Country of Mission,* was an important challenge to the Roman Catholic Church at the time, proposing that given the state of Christianity in France, it was in need of receiving missionaries more than sending them. Father Michineaux wrote *Revolution in the City Parish*, a widely read book about experimentation in city parish life. Also, during that post-war period, the Taize Community was founded in France, creating new forms of monastic disciplines for lay people, exploring creative liturgy and music, and reaching out to youth.

In Germany, students who were trained in Bonhoeffer's "Boxcar Seminary" explored new ministries after the war. Some, ordained by East German churches, worked as laborers in East German factories. In the postwar period, castles and chateaus that had been nationalized under the Nazis were given to the church and made into Evangelical Academies where lay people came together to reflect on the meaning of the Christian faith. Industries sent young apprentices to the Academies for moral and ethical formation.

In the spirit of these post-war experiments in new Christian forms of community, the East Harlem Protestant Parish was begun in New York City by a group of Union Seminary students. Some of them were veterans of the Second World War, who had gone to seminary after the war, but were not satisfied with the idea of following normal career paths in ministry. They undertook a study of the East Harlem community during their last year in seminary in an attempt to understand its dynamics, problems, and the role of the church there. They identified three blocks, said to be the most heavily populated blocks in New York, where the residents were predominantly African American and Puerto Rican. East 100th Street between First and Second Avenues was home to 4,000 people living in 800 apartment units. Those seminarians stood on both corners of the block for several Sundays to count the number of people who could conceivably be on their way to church. Their highest tally was ten. They were attracted to the challenge of starting a congregation in that community.

After graduating from seminary, they raised some money from various denominations and moved their families into East Harlem. The founding leaders were a diverse collection of strong characters. Don Benedict was a pacifist who had refused to register for the draft in WW II and spent time in prison. In reading the theologian Reinhold Niebuhr's books while incarcerated, he rethought his pacifist stance and embraced Niebuhr's "Christian realism". After getting out of jail, Benedict enlisted in the army and became a First Sergeant serving in the Pacific. Bill Webber had been a Navy officer during the war. There he met his wife Helen who was also in the Navy. After the war he went to Union Seminary. Archie Hargraves was one of the few black students at Union Seminary at the time. He was from the South and came to Union with a commitment to racial and social justice.

These three men and their families took up residence in East Harlem and comprised the core of the initial Group Ministry of the East Harlem Protestant Parish. They set up a card table to give out information and enroll kids in the neighborhood for a summer program. They rented a storefront space and ran a successful vacation church school geared to the interests of the children in that community. The experience also included field trips to places of interest in the city. Members of the team began to visit the families of the children, learning their stories, aspirations and concerns, and seeing if they might have interest in initiating a new faith community. They knocked on every door in each of the five or six-story tenement buildings.

Some of us at Yale visited this East Harlem group as it was starting up and decided that we should try a similar experiment in New Haven. Bob Forsberg and Joan Bates, who later became Joan Forsberg; Eugene "Jeep" Wolf and Lois, later his wife; and I began work in the Oak Street neighborhood, a low-income neighborhood adjacent to Yale University Hospital. The Forsbergs and the Wolfs stayed there and took up full-time ministry in that neighborhood when we graduated and I went on to New York. The neighborhood no longer exists because of the expansion of the Yale Hospital and Medical Center. The work continues under the name of the New Haven Wider City Ministry.

At the time I graduated, with my interest in urban ministry and the exploration of less traditional forms of Christian witness, it was a logical decision to join the EHPP, by then in existence for about two years. The founders were still recruiting others to join them in this experiment, which was coalescing around that Group Ministry in a kind of urban, familial monasticism. Spouses from the beginning were full and participating members of the Group. There was a shared conviction that members of a Group Ministry should reside in the community and that the Group Ministry should be shaped by a "rule of life" that included four disciplines – religious, economic, political and vocational.

The *Religious Discipline* meant that we as a group committed ourselves to a regular practice of individual and group worship and Bible study. Each one of our homes had a visible worship center, which was usually a cross, an open Bible and some candles. These worship centers provided an open witness to our faith as well as a gathering place for the reading of the daily lectionary. We also committed ourselves to a discipline of ongoing Bible study and theological reflection. The Group Ministry would gather at least one full day a month and sometimes overnight to reflect on our work through prayer and Bible study.

The *Economic Discipline* called for members of the group to share their fiscal resources. All of our assets were put into a common pot and the Group would collectively allocate to each family according to its needs. The economic communal sharing of the early Christian community described in the Book of Acts was our inspiration. On the income side, there were some of the Group members who had outside jobs and contributed their earnings to the Group. Others had inheritances, savings or properties to share. All members of the Group received their incomes from the common purse of the Group Ministry. After the community put all income on the table, each family would detail its financial needs. The Group then determined the amount allotted to each family. Whatever gap there was between the collective income and family expenses was what the EHPP itself had to raise through our emerging congregations, denominational support, and other fund-raising efforts. The divulging of each family's needs – how much we needed for food, housing, clothing, and even recreation – was sometimes more difficult than declaring income. We were not accustomed to opening up about such personal matters. As the Group Ministry grew, this practice of having as many as ten families sharing their economic resources and requirements was a distinctive and demanding aspect of the Group Ministry disciplines. The practice certainly stood in stark contrast to the trends in the wider American culture, which was increasingly individualistic and capitalistic.

The *Political Discipline* meant that we all accepted responsibility for addressing the needs of the community in political arenas. Direct services were a necessary part of the ministry, given the need, but we all believed that social change through political action was necessary for social justice. The Group supported particular candidates and took positions on specific issues. Some members of the Group ran for public office, such as City Council. Members did not publicly take positions differing from the Group without the consent of the Group.

The *Vocational Discipline* specified that in joining the Group Ministry the members committed themselves to East Harlem, to these disciplines and to the Group Ministry for as far ahead as they could see. This was not necessarily a life commitment, but neither was it a short-term involvement to get an "East Harlem experience" before moving on to other work. To join the Group Ministry was to covenant to ministry in East Harlem and to the other families involved. If one came to a time of considering another call, the discipline recognized that the decision to leave the Parish would not be only a private deliberation. One was obligated to hear reactions, reservations, counsel and advice from the Group. Ultimately, it was an individual's prerogative to leave and pursue what they perceived to be God's calling, but not before taking seriously the input of the community.

These four disciplines made for a rich context of mutual give and take, and a monitoring of one another's life and lifestyle as a background for the ministry itself. The Group Ministry was not an end in itself, but served the purposes of the larger community ministry. Practicing these disciplines made for tight interpersonal relationships and bound the men and women of the group together in ways that strengthened our work in the East Harlem community.

Most of those who worked and participated in the EHPP's work were not members of this Group Ministry. In retrospect, the Group Ministry concept had both strengths and weaknesses. On the positive side, it was an expression of the seriousness of their calling to those dedicated to the ministry, and more important, provided valuable mutual support for those engaged in living and working in a challenging situation. One of its weaknesses was the inevitable insider/outsider dynamic that emerged around such a tightly knit Group Ministry. This issue particularly came into play as members of the East Harlem community and the emerging congregations were assuming leadership roles. Early on in the EHPP, as congregations were organized, a Parish Council was established that included leadership from all the growing constituencies and institutions connected with the work. Some lay members, volunteers and student workers explored participating in some of the disciplines.

When I came to the Parish in June 1951, I had already been ordained as a Baptist Minister by Judson Church in 1950. With an aim of calling into being new congregations in East Harlem, the Group Ministry wanted to avoid owning church buildings that required a great deal of money and maintenance. Many urban congregations in low income communities were strapped with the cost of maintaining deteriorating facilities. The new EHPP congregations rented storefront spaces which the new members could afford to maintain. The large shop-front windows also made activities inside visible from the street. The space was the kind neighborhood residents were accustomed to using every day.

I moved into a 100th Street apartment and began knocking on my neighbors' doors. Although some people were hesitant to talk, many were willing to open their doors to have a conversation. We would share our commitment to living in the neighborhood and our desire to start a church. We asked them to share their ideas about what a church might look like that would be of interest to them. Some people were very hospitable, inviting us in for a cup of coffee, and opening up about their lives. If people showed interest in continuing the conversation, we would enlist them to host a meeting in their apartment with neighbors.

After a few months of intense visitation, there were some dozen small groups meeting on the block. Some met every week and others less frequently, but always with refreshments, singing, Bible study, discussion of family and community problems, and whether the Christian faith offered insights on those concerns. As people got to know each other better, they shared stories and found common ground. They often found themselves envisioning ways they themselves could act to make life in the community better.

Many of the families identified narcotics as a serious neighborhood problem. Two Group Ministry members, Norman and Peg Eddy, brought parents, addicts and dealers together to discuss what could be done about their kids becoming victims of the drug trade. People met regularly, agreed to keep confidentiality, and to talk about everything they knew about narcotics in the neighborhood. Out of this group's deliberations, a number of leaders wrote a play called *Dope*, which dramatized how a person got hooked on narcotics. It was performed during the summer in the vacant lots of the neighborhood. The first week *Dope* was presented, the baseball legend Jackie Robinson came to introduce the play. The script for the play was chosen for the annual Best One-Act Plays of the Year collection of 1951.

Through the Bible study groups and these community activities, a congregation came into existence and the leaders rented a storefront property. Community residents cleaned up the space, furnished it out, and created a chapel that became the 100th Street Church, East Harlem Protestant Parish.

As the ministry developed, a number of students were assigned to the Parish for their fieldwork from Union Theological Seminary. There were not too many women seminarians at the time, as most "mainline" denominations had not yet begun ordaining female clergy. When asked by a fieldwork placement supervisor what qualifications I wanted for an intern, I suggested, "How about marriageable?" Obligingly, the field assignment made by the seminary was a young woman named Kathleen Franklin who had started seminary in 1952. She worked closely with me during the school year and decided to stay on for the summer. She said, years later, in a memoir she wrote about our life together, that she found me "dashing." I appreciated her spirit and intelligence, as well as her beauty and charm.

Kathy came from a long Presbyterian heritage. Her parents were missionaries in Japan, working with the famous Japanese Christian leader, Toyohiko Kagawa. She was baptized as an infant by this Japanese modern-day saint. After their first five-year term, her parents had to leave the mission field because some church officials considered their missionary work in Japan, with issues like land reform and worker's rights, as "radical activities." Union Seminary theologian Reinhold Niebuhr, under whom her father had studied, asked him to become the staff director for the Delta Cooperative Farm in Mississippi. Niebuhr, along with Sherwood Eddy of the YMCA, had helped to start the farm in 1936 as a refuge for sharecroppers who were thrown off their land when they joined the Southern Tenant Farmers Union. Kathy spent a good part of her childhood and youth in that multi-racial cooperative setting in the Mississippi delta and its successor, the Providence Cooperative Farm, near Tchula, Mississippi. Later, in 1947, at the end of World War II, Kathy's parents were asked by their mission board to return to Japan where they remained another 20 years.

By mid-summer we had become engaged and were married in November of 1953. Since Reinhold Niebuhr was close to Kathy's parents, he performed our marriage ceremony in East Harlem. Kathy became a full member of the Group Ministry and we soon began a family.

There were strong bonds between EHPP and the faculty of Union Seminary, who found the East Harlem experiment interesting. Paul Tillich, Robert McAfee Brown and Reinhold Niebuhr provided regular encouragement and often met with Parish leaders.

Paul Tillich's ground-breaking theology had much influence in our thinking about the work. Tillich was critical of much of the earlier German theology that had informed Protestant thinking. In contrast to a special "heilsgeschichte," Tillich argued that all of history is holy history where God is present and active. What is happening right now, and what was happening in the history of other cultures and religions, are all within the framework of God's creative, loving, redeeming action. Tillich's idea of "autonomous culture" resists any understanding that holy history may belong exclusively to any one church or religion.

It is in that autonomous culture that the Spirit moves, and is always moving, not only bringing new things into being, but also leaving old things behind. By the end of the 20th century, Tillich said, the churches of the Reformation may have fulfilled their role in the divine plan, famously predicting "the end of the Protestant era." He expected that Reformation-founded churches might continue as museums into the next millennium for people devoted to that era's architecture, liturgy, and music. The Spirit will have moved on, bringing into being new forms.

By 1952, there were three thriving EHPP storefront churches that had been initiated. The Presbyterians also had a more traditional congregation in the neighborhood on 106th Street named the Church of the Ascension. It was barely surviving, as Judson Church had been, with only a handful of people, mainly of the neighborhood's remaining Italian Waldensian residents. The church was begun in early 20th century by Northern Italian immigrants who designed and built the church building with their own hands. One former pastor of the congregation had been Norman Thomas, the Presbyterian minister who became a perennial Socialist Party candidate for president. When the congregation celebrated its 50th anniversary in 1960, Norman Thomas came to preach and participate in the celebration.

The Parish and the Presbyterians got together and talked about the possibility of the Ascension congregation and building becoming part of EHPP as its fourth church. Some Presbyterian leadership had reservations about how a traditional congregation might fit into the parish and still maintain its Reformed identity. The Parish leadership was also uneasy about the collaboration because our storefront church strategy questioned taking on the responsibility of a historic church building. On the other hand, the Parish had enough participants and programs going – worship, house meetings, street actions, Christian education and summer camps – that it seemed attractive to have a space where all the congregations could gather in one place for celebrations, memorial services, big meetings and demonstrations. An agreement was reached between the Presbytery and the EHPP that I would be the one to provide pastoral leadership there.

With my marriage to Kathy, I was now ensconced in a staunch Presbyterian family and pastor of a historically Presbyterian congregation, so it made sense to respond to the Presbytery of New York's suggestion that I become a Presbyterian pastor. They recognized my American Baptist ordination and received me as a member of the presbytery in 1953.

An ongoing evolution in the Group Ministry was focused on how to open up the Group Ministry's decision-making and disciplines to the members of the congregations that were coming into being. Some families in the congregations wanted to participate in the disciplines that shaped the lives of the Group Ministry. Over time more and more Hispanic and African-American congregational leaders emerged to take their place at the decision-making table and shape the directions of the ministry, primarily through the formation of a Parish Council.

From the beginning, worship was at the center of Parish life. We paid careful attention to the aesthetics of worship. The Canon in charge of worship at the Cathedral of St. John the Divine helped us design vestments. We collected hymns and songs about the city and published a Parish songbook, edited by Mary Lou Taggart, a Group Ministry member. The new songbook included traditional hymns, gospel music, Hispanic songs, African-American spirituals, and some social justice movement songs. We developed a cycle of dramas for the Nativity, Three Kings Day, Shrove Tuesday, Mardi Gras, a Passion Play, an outdoor Easter sunrise service, and a Pentecost celebration.

Some of the things we did in worship were at that time innovative, at least for established Protestantism. We sang lots of gospel music and spirituals. This was before the black civil rights and black power movements of the sixties. Even so, we were singing "We Shall Overcome" which had not yet become an anthem of the Civil Rights movement. Everybody learned the Parish Purpose, taken from Jesus' first sermon in Luke 4:16-20, which the congregation repeated at every service: "The Spirit of the Lord is upon me because he has anointed me to preach the gospel to the poor, deliverance to the captives, recovering of sight to the blind, and to proclaim the year when all people may find acceptance with the Lord." There was an extended time for expressing concerns of the church, for people to voice their intercessions for loved ones who were ill, having marital or family problems, or a friend in jail, or to celebrate birthdays and anniversaries or important accomplishments. This has become a common practice in churches now, but then it was new for most Protestants accustomed to more traditional styles of worship.

The worship life also highlighted the significance of baptism, marriage, and funerals. In baptism, the church declares that this is not just a baby, possibly born into a difficult situation, but this is a child of God, created in God's image, with infinite possibilities for fulfilling God's intention for this life. The congregation accepts responsibility for the intentions God has for this beloved one. Baptism becomes an event of celebration, sacralizing this new person who is becoming part of this community of God's people. Marriage becomes a celebration of the creation of a new family, the joining together of two families, and confirms the new family now assuming its role in the life of the community.

Funerals celebrated the valued life of someone who was part of the community. This was in contrast to the attitude that lives of people in communities like ours were sometimes not regarded as valuable. There was a great deal of violence in East Harlem. Young people were killed by gangs and also by the police. Special attention was given to victims of such violence, as well as to the family and community in mourning and shock. Although a person might be poor and their accomplishments humble, this was a person of God's creation, who was loved as part of the community. Making the liturgy support these Christian affirmations about life was an important part of the worship life of the Parish.

Many youth were attracted to the storefront churches and participated actively in its programs. On Friday, Saturday and Sunday nights there were big youth events. On Friday and Saturday nights there were very well attended community dances. On Sunday evenings at Church of the Ascension, youth from the several churches of the Parish gathered for Youth Worship. This became a popular event with more than 200 participating regularly. The minister-composer Al Carmines, then a student at Union, brought his trombone and several friends to make a jazz ensemble. The famous artist Jacob Lawrence came there to speak, as well as James Baldwin, who had just published his book of essays, *Fire Next Time.*

Early on, Bill Webber initiated a "Long Trail" tradition in the East Harlem Protestant Parish. Boys and girls of the Parish were taken out for a two or three-day backpack hiking trip on the Appalachian Trail. They slept in tents and cooked their own meals as they hiked the trails. There were remarkable changes going on for kids, many of whom had never been out of the city. Strong attachments were built between the kids and their leaders from this experience together.

House meetings, which began in the initial outreach period, always included Bible study, the Eucharist (the bread and wine of a simple communion), and sharing of concerns about community and personal problems. They continued through the whole history of the Parish.

There were Parish campaigns going on constantly. It became an annual event to have a clean-up day to dramatize the perennial problem of sanitation. Garbage pick-up was irregular and inadequate. There were clean-up days when the whole neighborhood would turn out with brushes and brooms and shovels. The Sanitation Department provided us with equipment. We'd clean up vacant lots and air shafts between buildings and the streets. The workforce would sing to the tune of the *Beer Barrel Polka*:

"Sweep, sweep East Harlem, we've got the dirt on the run.
Sweep, sweep East Harlem, our job has just now begun.
Stop airmail garbage, because it fouls the air,
Now's the time to use the trash cans – and that's why they're there!"

There was also ongoing tension with the police. Some patrolmen might take young people into the precinct headquarters, hold their heads in the toilet and flush, to secure a confession. Also, some police were "on the take" for narcotics trade. It was not uncommon to see a patrol car slow down at a corner, where someone would come out from a building and lean on the window of the police car. Money would clearly change hands and the police car would roll on.

The Parish was often in conflict with the police around treatment of residents and police corruption. One controversy resulted in the Precinct Commander being transferred. The new Precinct Commander was also a Baptist minister who served a church. Soon after he took office, he invited EHPP pastors to come to his office to meet with him. He said, "On this corner of my desk is the book of police regulations of the City of New York. I have to run the precinct under the rules of this book. On that other corner of my desk is the Bible. As a Christian, I want to be conducting our work by the teachings of this book." He opened the Bible and read to us two passages. The first was from Romans 13, about being obedient to the law. The Commander said, "Paul instructs us to pay our taxes because the tax collector is an agent of God, as are other governing authorities. Persons with authority have that authority from God. Like all authorities, the police have a responsibility to use their power responsibly." He then turned to the passage from Luke 3:12-14, about John the Baptist preaching in the wilderness with people coming out to see him. Among those who came were some soldiers asking, "What must we do to be saved?" John tells them, "Do not extort money from anyone by threats or false accusation and be content with your wages." The Commander declared, "I take this to mean for police: don't lie and don't take bribes." In this fascinating and concrete way, this precinct commander, a man of faith, was actualizing what theologians were suggesting about how God governs the structures of the world for the well-being of humanity.

Other EHPP concerns were affordable housing and job training for youth. One of our pastors, George Calvert, wanted to support himself and not be dependent on either EHPP subsidy or the members of his congregation, so he took a job as a bus driver. On the 104th Street block, where Calvert's Church of the Living Hope was located, the congregation bought a four-story tenement building. They redesigned and remodeled the ground floor into a handsome chapel. The upper floors were a manse for George and his family and residences for other members of the church. The Church of the Living Hope initiated a much bigger housing rehabilitation program in that block and throughout East Harlem. The congregation arranged to have their streets closed for block parties. At the corner of 104th Street and Third Avenue the congregation enlisted an artist to paint on a brick wall a mural with portraits of dozens of residents on the block engaged in their everyday family and vocational activities.

When the Police Department built new headquarters, it turned its old precinct building over to the Church of the Living Hope for one dollar a year to be the headquarters of the Living Hope Community which served the whole block. They effectively organized tenants to buy their buildings, rehab them with sweat equity and make them into co-ops. George Calvert's son, David, organized a citywide youth employment program and trained hundreds of young people in East Harlem in building trade skills. They transformed dozens of buildings in different parts of East Harlem over a ten-year period.

During the 1960s, another significant effort was called Metro North. The Parish helped to organize a group of residents who employed planning professionals to work for and with the community to develop a comprehensive plan for the future of East Harlem. The plan has been implemented over the past 20 years, producing many blocks of rehabilitated apartments and new buildings.

Another interesting aspect of life in the Parish was the on-going conversation with other experimental forms of Christian community taking place throughout the world. George McLeod, leader of the Iona Community in Scotland, visited the Parish several times to see its work and share with EHPP stories about the urban ministry efforts in Glasgow. We also received visitors from urban and industrial efforts in other countries and from other states. Members of the Parish also visited those experiments to see what could be learned and brought back to East Harlem. The East Harlem Parish became recognized as one of a number of model urban ministries emerging throughout the world at that time. It served as a model for urban parishes initiated in New Haven, Cleveland, Chicago, and Denver, and helped to stimulate increased attention to ministry in cities by churches all over the country.

One of the tensions the Parish had to wrestle with over time was the question of becoming more institutionalized and at the same time staying organizationally flexible. This came to the fore when a large financial gift came to the Parish and we had to decide how to use it. Some felt the Group should buy a building with it. They believed that since EHPP had been in existence for ten years, it was time for us to have something more permanent. They asked, "What do we have to show for all our work?" If we had a building, they argued, we could have proper office space and places where people could hold meetings and carry programs beyond what storefronts could hold.

Some of us countered that getting into the building business was contrary to EHPP'S basic strategy from the beginning. Our storefronts were in the midst of the community and maintained by the church members' own resources. That space was theirs. This new property would not belong to the people in the same way. It would require time and resources to be maintained that would be drained from our current community based activities. The discussion went round and round, but eventually a decision was made to purchase a building. This action factored eventually into the decision Kathy and I made to leave East Harlem.

In that debate, I was not willing to concede that it is a sociological necessity for a movement that springs from the Spirit's action in the world to become institutionalized. In Richard Niebuhr's book, *The Social Sources of Denominationalism*, he illustrates well the tendency of Protestant churches to evolve from being movements of the Spirit into institutions with constitutions and by-laws, officers, and structures. I do not believe this is inevitable that a spirit-driven congregation must become a program-absorbed institution. EHPP had the possibility of remaining the kind of body that was spirit-filled and did not have to experience a "hardening of the arteries." The decision to purchase a building with an unexpected foundation grant was disappointing to me.

Over the years the EHPP attracted a certain amount of publicity. There appeared several magazine articles (*e.g. the New Yorker* and *The Saturday Evening Post)* and the books *Island in the City* by Dan Wakefield, *Come Out the Wilderness* by Bruce Kendrick and *My People is the Enemy* by William Stringfellow.

Bill Stringfellow and I became friends while we were both involved with the World Student Christian Federation in the 1940s. After college he was drafted and spent time in the occupation army in Germany following the Second World War. After his tour of duty he went to Harvard Law School. Bill was a deeply committed Christian and thoughtful critical thinker and was soon publishing articles relating his Biblical and theological insights to the social issues around him. He and I had stayed in touch and he came to visit the Parish. After getting his law degree and trying to discern his vocation, he decided to come to the Parish as a lawyer and moved into a tenement on East 100th Street. During his stay, Bill used his skills to assist Parish residents with their legal problems. He later wrote his book, *My People is the Enemy*, as a reflection on his experience of living and working in East Harlem.

In 1958 the Parish decided to institute sabbaticals for members of the Group Ministry, enabling them to take three or four months off every six years. Since Kathy and I had already been with the EHPP for almost eight years, our sabbatical opportunity came up rather quickly. The Presbyterian Overseas Mission Board had been talking to us for a couple of years about the possibility of traveling in Asia to help them identify Christian communities that were doing work similar to ours. "Where are the East Harlem Protestant Parishes in some of the Asian churches?" was their question.

We agreed to use our sabbatical for such a trip. I was somewhat resistant to what was going to be an important element of the journey. The Board wanted me to visit Taiwan and talk about urban ministry at the Tainan

Theological Seminary. Taiwan had been occupied by Chiang Kai-Shek when Mao Tse-Tung came to power in China. Chiang had instituted a military dictatorship supported by the United States government, calling Taiwan "Free China," in juxtaposition to the Communist mainland. I was reluctant to be involved with a country where I thought U.S. policy was so wrong.

At this time the Presbyterians had initiated something they called "industrial evangelism" (sometimes called urban-industrial or urban or industrial, and sometimes using the word "mission.") This work was pioneered through the distinguished missionary service of Henry Jones, a missionary in Shanghai laboring among factory workers. After the Communist takeover, he managed to work in China for another four years, before relocating to Japan, where he continued his work with Asian churches, encouraging them in their ministry to migrants in growing industrial cities. To my surprise, my lecture assignment at the seminary went very well and the students were very interested in the discussion of the church's engagement in the growing urbanization and industrialization of their society. The seminary president, Dr. C.H. Whang, asked if I would consider coming to teach at his school full time and was prepared to request support from the Presbyterian Mission Board. Though appreciative of his offer, I was fully intending to return to my work in the EHPP with renewed energy and commitment.

In the few months of our sabbatical, the Parish had moved further down the road of institutionalizing program and was focused on the development of the building that had been purchased. Some of the original EHPP pioneers had already gone at this point and I felt increasingly at odds with the directions of the ministry. I sensed it was time to leave and the opportunity to teach in Asia through the Presbyterian Mission Board seemed to be a way to share the experience of EHPP in a new setting. Kathy and I took the idea to the Group Ministry, as the discipline required, and after consideration they concurred. By this time we had three preschool sons – John, Peter and Sam. Sam was just a few months old. We thought an overseas experience could be exciting for them as well. After all, Kathy had been pre-schooled in Japan as a child of missionaries.

One of the challenges the Parish faced over time was the inherent difficulty of a predominantly white group of leaders who initiated the Parish and stayed in central leadership roles over time. With the emerging consciousness of black empowerment in the 1960s, it was appropriate that the leadership of EHPP change as well. The congregations in the Parish each took on a denominational identity and continue to this day. The Group Ministry and the East Harlem Protestant Parish itself were officially dissolved in the 1970s.

In 1998, several hundred people gathered in East Harlem to celebrate the 50th anniversary of the founding of the Parish. The gathering included many of the original members of the Group Ministry, former pastors of the congregations, dozens of the more than 300 seminarians who had done field work in EHPP, large numbers of people from the community, and leadership from the city who came to acknowledge the importance of the EHPP in the community. There were moving testimonials of ways in which the work of the Parish changed lives, deepened faith, built lifelong friendships, shaped vocations, brought solace and healing, inspired new forms of the church, and revitalized a neighborhood. My colleague, Trey Hammond, in writing about the gathering in an article entitled "East of Harlem" in the *Monday Morning* publication of the Presbyterian Church, noted, "A couple of questions from the reunion have troubled me. First, where are the comparably bold experiments in new Christian community taking place today? Even though the limitations of the current form of congregational life are all too apparent, we seem to be more comfortable in tinkering with the known rather than experimenting with new structures. Second, where is the church living out a fundamental critique of the values of ascendant capitalism and individualism? The disciplines of the EHPP outlined a Christian communitarian existence that was subversive by its very incarnation. East of Harlem – the imagery is evocative. That is where we are now, trying to live out God's witness in the post-modern city. The questions posed by the East Harlem Protestant Parish still beg for answers."

Kathy and I left the Parish in August, 1959. As Kathy wrote some years later, "Our days and nights were filled with meetings and services, weddings, baptisms and funerals, daily vacation Bible school for neighborhood children in the summers, youth recreational programs, drug clinics, hospital visits, political demonstrations, and the frequent personal crises of our parishioners. I now treasure those years for the friends we made who showed us how to live with dignity and faith when life is harsh and unpredictable." We ended our time there deeply thankful for all that the Parish had meant to us and eager to experience a new ministry and continent to which we were being led.

# CHAPTER 3

— ❧ —

# An Asian Sojourn: The Taiwan Experience (1959-1963)

WE ARRIVED AT the Tainan Theological College at the beginning of a semester. It was a new world for us, living in this ancient culture, surrounded by the 300 Buddhist and animist temples in Tainan. In Taiwan, like many industrializing nations, thousands of young men and women from farms and villages were coming to work in newly established industries in rapidly growing cities. Tainan was the original capital city of Taiwan, established when the Ming dynasty was driven from China by the Manchus more than 300 years earlier. In 1959, following World War II, more than 60 years of Japanese occupation had ended. A large American air base covered many acres on the edge of the city. With American development aid, dozens of new factories had been started. Tainan reflected this dynamic mixture of old and new cultures. I remember how thrilled our boys were when bicycle-cabs transported us from the airport through the busy streets of the city to the seminary.

The Taiwanese Presbyterian Church was one of the largest Christian churches in Asia. Tainan Theological College was founded in 1876 by British missionaries and was one of two seminaries for the Taiwanese Presbyterian Church. By the time we arrived the faculty had transitioned from missionary faculty to mostly Taiwanese professors. The school had an enrollment of some 300 students. We settled into our new living quarters, one of the cottages provided for faculty members on the seminary campus.

We started the challenging task of learning the Amoy dialect of Chinese. Fortunately, my teaching was not dependent upon my fluency.

In advanced classes, the students were skilled in English and in other settings skilled interpreters translated the lectures. My task was to help equip a body of local leaders, who were knowledgeable of their own context, with tools for on-going social analysis, and to encourage their imagination for inventing the church's mission response to a society rapidly changing from being rural and agricultural to becoming urban and industrial. My colleagues in this task were the faculty in the seminary and the students themselves. My contribution to their dialogue was the experience of the urban industrial ministry work in America's most urban context, New York City, and the insights of experiments in new missional forms such as Judson Church and the East Harlem Protestant Parish.

There were some challenges needing to be addressed in the school. The college offered a six-year curriculum leading to a degree in theology. The first years covered basic college subjects, with theology and practice of ministry emphasized in the last three years. "Christian Ethics" had never been offered as a distinct discipline in the curriculum, nor had "Social Ethics." New course outlines were generated and I began to offer courses in *Christian Ethics, Church and Society, Social Ethics, The Church and Economic Life*, and *Christianity and Marxism.* That last class quickly caught the attention of the local government intelligence office. Some of their agents became regular auditors of that course. Much of the curriculum was drawn from the academic discourse at Yale and Union, the ongoing theological reflection inside the East Harlem Protestant Parish, and course work I had taken at Columbia Graduate School of Social Work in community organization. In introducing Tainan students to community organizing, I found it useful to have Saul Alinsky's *Reveille for Radicals* translated into Chinese.

My course on *The Church and Economic Life* was offered every semester and was largely drawn from my undergraduate major in economics. Fortunately, there were a couple of textbooks that well described the economic forces at work in urbanizing and industrializing societies. Topics included the sources of capital for investment in industry and the need for new skills development for the large numbers of people moving from agricultural labor into an industrial workforce. We considered questions of justice, in relationship to how the profits from economic development should be distributed, and the appropriate role of the government in redistributing income.

A second area of challenge in the seminary was the revamping of the supervised fieldwork program. It had previously been a rather informal process. The names of the students were put in one hat and the names of churches requesting student assistance in another. One faculty member would draw out student names and another would pick out the name of a congregation. These assignments were posted on a bulletin board. There would be two or three days of brokering among the churches and the students seeking to switch. When the field work began, there was little in the way of reflection on the work experiences. We initiated a more intentional placement system and an ongoing support program for the students in their field placements, to encourage correlation between classroom learning and the work in their congregational assignment.

What emerged was a plan for two years of required supervised fieldwork in their six-year program, which combined college and seminary. One year took place in a congregation as a "church-directed" experience and the other year's assignment was in work outside the context of a congregation in "world-directed" experience. All of the members of the faculty were recruited to participate in the supervision of the students, along with the participating pastors. A team of two or three faculty would meet weekly with small groups of students to discuss what they were doing in their field placements.

A series of assignments was developed for the church-directed internships. For example, exercises included:

- Draw a map of ten square blocks surrounding the church and identify the residences, businesses and shops;
- Do a social breakdown analysis of the membership and constituency of the congregation as to age, sex, occupation and social class;

- Write a history of the congregation; how and when was the congregation founded, and who made up the current congregation;
- Interview church members and talk to people in the community who are not related to the church to see what impressions they have of the church; what image did the church have among its own members and in the community?
- Is it possible to characterize what the members of the congregation believe? Talk to members and to each officer of the church to find out the key aspects of their Christian faith; what was most meaningful to them in their participation as members?
- We declare that Jesus Christ is Lord over all principalities, powers, and dominions. What is the meaning of that for the relationship of the church to "principalities, powers and dominions" of the community where this congregation is located?

The assignments often involved church members and stimulated their own analysis of their congregational contexts. Overall, the faculty was supportive of this new approach to fieldwork. These exercises helped congregations understand themselves and communities in ways that gave them new perspectives on their own mission and ministry.

Another major focus of my time was the development of the "world-directed" field-work assignments. We tried to create experiences which might enhance skills of seminarians to better understand their own communities and evoke ways their congregations could minister beyond the walls of their church buildings.

Given the explosive growth of industry, one important arena of field placements involved employing seminarians in factories, where they experienced the life of workers firsthand. Many workers lived in factory compounds in barracks provided by the employers. The seminarians, using skills they had acquired in school for working with young people, were welcomed when they came to the dorms offering recreation, classes, discussion groups, and music to workers new to the city. Through these contacts and friendships students came to know about the realities of life on the factory floor. Students also got exposed to the relationships between workers and the owners and managers of the factories.

Some students interned in labor unions. Here they explored some basics of labor organizing and how labor unions might best represent the interest of workers. Also, the city government opened up places for students to participate in municipal offices such as housing, planning, and public health.

One unusual field setting was in a busy marketplace about a block from the seminary. At the intersection was a large traffic circle with the market in the center, providing space for vendors selling clothing, books, medicine, groceries, and colorful foods, such as snake soup brewed on an open fire. Some students took on field placements in the market, working for vendors, and sharing the challenges of shop keeping and customer service. Other students rented a stall and ran a bookstore, learning firsthand the challenge of running a small business. The interns became familiar with the Market Association and its role in advocating for small business people with the government and the police. They interacted with customers and learned what interested them. In the center of the marketplace, there was an entertainment space that featured storytellers, hand puppeteers, drama troupes, singers, and mimes. Students joined in the entertainment, singing, and performing with puppets. This was a popular field assignment. The market was always crowded, day and night, and was an exciting place to work and learn.

There were other more traditional institutional settings, such as a mental hospital and a juvenile detention center. One of the daily newspapers agreed to intern a couple of students. The paper's editors and I negotiated an understanding of the scope of the work, which was twofold. First, they would give higher profile to church news by publicizing congregational activities. Second, we wanted the interns to have the latitude to enhance the newspaper's coverage of matters of justice and human need. The churches were delighted to see the increased coverage of church efforts, while, with participation of the students, issues such as housing, labor grievances, juvenile justice, public health, prostitution and sexual exploitation, and other justice concerns would get higher profile in the paper. The paper ran an expose of the scandalous conditions in a local mental hospital, spearheaded by our students, with the cause then taken up by more senior reporters. The students' journalism gave the church new ideas on directions its ministry could take in relation to society and enhanced ethical conscience in ongoing reporting undertaken by the paper.

In addition to the regular school year field placements, we also offered summer work/study courses. The program was modeled after Marshall Scott's *Students-in-Industry* program in Chicago which had for decades placed seminarians and clergy in factory workplace settings. The students rented a *tatami* apartment, a one-room, working-class lodging with straw mats for sleeping, eating, and meeting. Jobs were secured in steel mills, plastic, textile, papermaking, shoe, and other manufacturing plants. They would have an eight to ten week experience of working as full-time laborers in these factories. Owners, managers, labor leaders, government officials, clergy, and professors were enlisted to meet with the group for reflections. We would eat supper together, discuss their daily experience, and share Bible study on the nature of work, the dignity of the person, and scripture's teaching on just economic life. Such sessions ended with prayers and the sharing of Eucharist, bread and wine, as we sat on the floor of the *tatami* room. These intense summer experiences deeply bonded the students and the faculty and were often life changing times for the participants.

During one school year, a couple of students in world-directed fieldwork envisioned using hand puppets, traditionally employed for Buddhist Temple celebrations, to dramatize Bible stories in the streets. They enlisted one of the well-known puppet companies in the project. The master puppeteer used some of his puppets and made some new ones. He taught the students the art of puppet making and trained them in manipulating them. The shows were performed with a kind of Punch and Judy liveliness, raucous dialogue, and rambunctious staging. A band played traditional musical instruments to provide background music for different scenes, with fireworks added for exciting sequences. With the students, they staged versions of the Prodigal Son and the sacrifice of Isaac, along with other dramatic Biblical stories. Later the Taiwanese Presbyterian General Assembly sponsored an on-going traveling troupe, led by those *Student-In-Industry* puppeteers.

Though my primary responsibility was at the seminary, another aspect of my assignment involved working with the Taiwanese national Presbyterian Church offices and its presbyteries and congregations in thinking about the implications of urbanization and industrialization for the church. A number of presbyteries established committees to work on this venture and part of my job was to staff these committees. We would strategize on how each presbytery might look at their specific situation of industrialization and urban growth and how the individual churches might study demographic change in their own communities. We explored the possibilities of ministry to the large migrations of new workers coming into the city with their needs for housing, jobs, and spiritual sustenance.

Some of these presbyteries built upon this work in planning for new church development. At least five congregations seeded satellite con-gregations in growing population centers around new industrial develop-ment zones, typically on the edge of a city. One presbytery formed the Kaohsiung Church Labor Center for contact and ongoing dialogue with labor union leaders. It was directed by a clergy-person who had gradu-ated from the seminary and felt his calling was to facilitate an ongoing conversation between church and labor in Kaohsiung, a port and steel mill city.

Another area of focus with the national church revolved around the vocations of lay people. We would bring together people from a par-ticular vocational field such as civil service workers, teachers in public schools, people in the legal fields, or health care providers. They would discuss the challenges and possibilities of their callings and try to under-stand their work through the lens of faith.

In one occupational census of the congregations in a presbytery, we discovered a large number of barbers. The presbytery sponsored a conference for Presbyterian barbers and beauticians, to explore their vocation and their faith. We discussed the Reformed understanding of the priesthood of all believers that God has intentions in calling people to their various vocations. If such a vocational premise is true, what might be the intentions of a God who creates, governs, judges, and redeems for those called to the job of barbering? At that conference, the women and men barbers decided that perhaps God had called them to "help people be clean and beautiful." They talked about the joys and problems they experienced as Christians in their vocations. They struggled with the fact that sometimes barbershop waiting rooms were fronts for prostitution. Barbershops could often be places of rough language, arenas for gossip, and the display of questionable literature. In the context of their identity as Christians, they reflected on their daily work and thought through the difficulties they might face if they made their workplaces more reflective of their values and God's purposes.

The political climate during these years was tense and challenging. General Chiang Kai-shek held the reins of power in a dictatorial style, supported by a strong military. He was bolstered by the United States' anti-communist foreign policy. The Taiwan Presbyterian Church, about 250,000 strong, was a thorn in the side of the government and was regularly under surveillance, including the seminary.

All through the 1960's, Presbyterian churches were considered by the government to be centers of resistance. Even though the Taiwanese language was forbidden for public speaking, teaching, or publishing, Presbyterian pastors preached in Taiwanese and used Bibles and hymnbooks in the Taiwanese language. Some clergy were arrested and Taiwanese Bibles and church-published books were confiscated. The effort to suppress the traditional Taiwanese language and culture was a clear effort by the Chiang Kai-shek government to assert the political and cultural superiority of the mainland Chinese culture they imported when they fled to Taiwan, after the rise to power of Mao Tse-Tung in 1949.

Some church people and students were nervous when we approached government offices to serve as field study settings for students to work and learn. Even in the most bureaucratic setting, where one might expect to find deep cynicism and resistance, it was surprising to see doors open if genuine interest was expressed. People dropped their defenses when they were visited by citizens who were really interested in what they were doing, what their hopes and dreams were about their work, and what were some of their headaches and problems. Even relationships with police and intelligence agents relaxed when they felt they were being respected as human beings trying to do their best in their jobs.

We also had relationships with political activists, who were often perceived by the government as radical and subversive. During the time we were there, Taipei University professor Peng Mien Ming was arrested, suspended from the university, and placed under house arrest. After a period of time, he was allowed to take walks without guards. Sometimes I was able to meet with him surreptitiously to explore his options and to encourage him. Arrangements were made to get him out of the country using a forged passport. With the help of Amnesty International, as well as friendly contacts inside airport security, he was able to get to Hong Kong and to a safe haven in Oslo, where Kathy and I visited him later. Eventually, he became a professor in an American university. When things opened up politically in Taiwan, he returned and in 1996 ran for President. He was not elected, but his candidacy represented the huge political changes taking place in Taiwan.

One interesting project illustrated the desire of the Taiwanese not only to have the freedom to sing in their own language, but to find home-grown Christian music in Asia and not be reliant on the hymnody they received from the missionaries. One seminary student, Loh Ito, pursued a graduate degree in musical anthropology and, with sponsorship by the Christian Conference of Asia, traveled to many neighboring countries collecting hymns and songs. These were published in a new hymnal with songs from seventy two different languages from fifteen Asian countries.

I became increasingly uneasy about my role, and the role of other foreign missionaries, in Taiwan. For the witness of the church to go forward in Asia, there needed to be a moratorium on European and American up-front leadership as evangelists. It was time for the autonomous Asian churches to assume leadership and move forward, with American and European churches helping to support indigenous leadership.

This is not a critique of the missionaries. Many missionaries we knew were outstanding and talented people who were sensitive to these issues. Nevertheless, the clothes we wore and the houses we lived in were out of sync with the sermons we preached. Among the missionaries it was normal to have full-time childcare, a full-time cook, a full-time maid, and even a gardener, which were comparable amenities enjoyed in other upper-income professional fields in Taiwan. The huge differential in pay scale between local personnel and foreign missionaries spoke volumes.

COEMAR (Commission on Ecumenical Mission and Relations) was the agency inside the Presbyterian Church responsible for its relationships with churches in other countries. They had already begun a fundamental rethinking of their approach to international mission. After World War II, former Asian and African colonies had become independent. The missionary-initiated churches had become autonomous and were no longer "missions" of European and North American denominational bodies.

The Presbyterian Mission Board initiated an Advisory Study process which carried out consultative visits with every church with which Presbyterians had historic relationships. The study was brought to an assembly of representatives from all the churches historically receiving missionaries and funds. From these deliberations, four recommendations were brought to Presbyterian Mission Board and the General Assembly. These recommendations became the official policy of the church.

1.  Missionaries would no longer be sent abroad except by express invitation of partner churches. The traditional five year appointments would only be renewed upon invitation of those churches. Implementation of this policy, between 1962 and 1972, led to the reduction of the Presbyterian U.S.A. missionary force from 1,400 to 400.

2. Assistance to the partner churches should be given in block grants to enable those churches to define and carry out their own program priorities.

3. Some funds should be directed toward leadership training and development allowing the newly autonomous churches to equip skilled personnel to serve as pastors, seminary professors, teachers in schools and universities, administrators, and doctors. The partner church was free to design those training opportunities and choose participants.

4. Use overseas missionary resources to encourage and undergird ecumenical institutions and structures. Many national councils of churches were strengthened or came into being through implementation of this policy. The funding played a major role in strengthening regional bodies such as the Christian Conference of Asia, the All Africa Conference of Churches and three similar bodies in Latin America.

All of these considerations were going on during the time we were in Taiwan. We struggled with questions about the role of a missionary, the impact of colonialism, the coercive role of the U.S. foreign policy in Asia, and the question of American affluence and power. Our three-year term was extended one more year. The Taiwanese Presbyterian Church encouraged us to stay for another term, but we declined. COEMAR then urged us to take another assignment in the Middle East, but we had become even more strongly convinced that the foreign missionary era was over for North Americans. We decided not to pursue another overseas mission assignment.

A major part of our work in Taiwan was with professors, ministers, and students who were seeking ways to be more responsive to their context. It was time for Kathy and me to return to our home "context" in the United States and work at our calling there. With the birth of our son Adam in Taiwan, we now had four sons. The oldest was in grade school and the youngest in diapers. As appreciative as we were that they could experience the rich Chinese culture, we wanted our sons to spend some part of their childhood in America.

My expectation was to return to congregational ministry in an urban setting. I had tried to make contacts with presbyteries to explore possibilities of local pastorates. That was difficult to do from overseas. No calls from any congregations had come as the time came nearer for our departure. Then unexpected doors were opened through the work of a U.S. colleague, Marshall Scott.

Marshall Scott was a highly regarded leader in the Presbyterian Church. He was elected the moderator of the General Assembly while we were in Taiwan. He was founder and director of the Presbyterian Institute of Industrial Relations (PIIR) based in Chicago.

As the current elected Moderator of the Presbyterian Church USA, he traveled to Japan, South Korea, Taiwan, the Philippines and Hong Kong. When he came to Taiwan, I was given the responsibility of coordinating his visit. There were two large conferences where leadership from across the Taiwanese church was in attendance. I was able to arrange for Marshall to address both gatherings. Unbeknownst to me, a position had opened up in the Presbyterian Board of National Missions for the position of Director of the Urban and Industrial Mission Office. When Marshall returned from his tour, he recommended my name for the job.

Soon after, I was surprised to receive a letter asking if I might be interested in applying. I was skeptical at first. While I was working for the Parish at the Ascension Presbyterian Church in New York City, my official employer was the Board of National Missions of the Presbyterian Church. I had found the experience of relating to a church bureaucracy quite frustrating. I could not quite conceive of myself in a national church staff position. I was eager to return to an inner-city urban parish setting.

However, Kathy and I thought it might be an advantageous place from which to look for a job. I put down some of my ideas about what somebody in a national position for urban and industrial mission might do, and suggested that if this was what the job entailed, then I would be interested in more fully exploring the possibility. Less than a month later, a letter arrived. The gist was, "Could you report for work on the first of July?" Though surprised by the invitation, we said yes. We did not yet have a job description, know what the salary would be, or have any housing arrangements, but we were excited to return to New York. Nor could we possibly know the crises which were looming on the horizon for our nation and church in the tumultuous days of the 1960's. Nor could I foresee that I would be working in large church institutional structures for the next 20 years.

# CHAPTER 4

— ⚗ —

# Living Through the Sixties: Urban Industrial Ministry in the United Presbyterian Church USA (1963-1972)

I REPORTED FOR work at the Presbyterian Board of National Missions offices at the Interchurch Center in New York the first week of July 1963 and joined a rich history of urban ministry in the United Presbyterian Church in the U.S.A. That history stretches back to the beginnings of the Presbyterian Church in the 1500s under the leadership of John Calvin. Reformed theology and practice has strongly emphasized the role of the church in shaping the civic order. Calvin's church in Geneva engaged deeply in shaping the quality of the life of the city. Constitutional and civil institutions were developed, intended to insure the common good. The Presbyterian Church's role in American life has also been significant. American Presbyterians were catalysts in shaping the democratic constitutional underpinnings of the emerging republic. Several Presbyterians participated in the writing of the American constitution and were among the original signers of the Declaration of Independence. In the 18th and 19th centuries American Presbyterians were actively involved in founding education, health care and social service institutions necessary to assure their society's well-being.

The Department of Urban and Industrial Ministry (UIM) was founded in 1907 under the name Office for Immigrant and Industrial Work. Thousands of immigrant families from Europe were landing at New York's Ellis Island to be processed for admission to the United States. The Board of National Missions committed itself to welcoming new residents from Italy, Ireland, Scotland, Germany, and Eastern European countries that crowded into the Lower East Side and from there migrated to other urban areas throughout the country. The first director of the office was Rev. Charles Stetzle. One of his first purchases was a portable foot-pump organ which he carried to Ellis Island for Sunday services with the new immigrants. Czech, Italian, Hungarian, Chinese, and Scottish immigrants founded Presbyterian congregations in New York City and other urban areas.

In 1914 a mission congregation was begun with the aim of reaching out to and serving the low income and working families of the crowded Lower East Side. Many immigrants were working in factories with unsafe conditions and low wages. Newly organizing labor unions found landlords unwilling to rent space to them for offices and meetings. The new church took the name "Labor Temple" and offered office and meeting space for the struggling organizers. That congregation became a vibrant community center offering English language classes, Bible studies, political and social study groups, sports programs and cultural events, as well as Christian education and worship services. The Labor Temple continued its ministry into the late 1940s. Stetzle's leadership was visionary and not without controversy. The Labor Temple was an active part of the Social Gospel Movement which was influencing the theology and ethics of mainline denominations in the first quarter of the century in the belief that, along with calling individuals into personal relationship with God, the church needed to call institutions into alignment with God's purposes for society.

New urban efforts emerged over several decades as the church took seriously the mission of addressing the needs of newcomers struggling to make a new life in growing cities and expanding industries across the country. The Presbyterian Institute of Industrial Relations (PIIR), founded in 1944 and based in the Labor Temple, was a program for equipping clergy and students preparing for ministry to understand and work among industrial workers and their families and communities. PIIR annually offered three-week residential seminars for pastors introducing them to business, political and labor leaders. The training included field trips to factories and workers' tenements, exploring ways that churches could serve the interests of working people. Each summer, from 20 to 30 seminary students were recruited and placed in shop-floor industrial jobs. These *Students-in-Industry* would gather after work to engage in Bible study and theological reflection on their work and to speak with business and labor leaders. PIIR moved to Chicago and continued this work in conjunction with McCormick Seminary. By 1986, it was estimated that more than 4,000 of the 9,000 USA Presbyterian pastors had been exposed to labor issues through PIIR programs.

Starting in the late 19th century, the Presbyterian Church established a number of settlement houses and community centers which provided support for new immigrant populations in urban areas. These centers offered an array of services – Boy and Girl Scouts, sports, English classes, health and counseling programs, job training, tutoring, and parent support groups. Some centers actively mobilized their members and neighbors to work for better schools, hospitals, and police protection. Two of those well-known houses were Cameron House in San Francisco's China Town and Erie House in a multi-ethnic neighborhood in Chicago.

Another part of the Urban Ministry legacy was the development and support of racial-ethnic congregations. In the years during and after World War II there was a huge migration of African Americans from southern rural communities seeking employment in northern cities. Before and after the Civil War a number of African-American Presbyterian congregations were founded in the South along with a number of African-American schools and colleges. Immigrants to northern cities soon established many new black congregations in the North. They were often housed in church buildings vacated by white congregations that had moved as neighborhoods changed. The national church and its Presbyteries provided resources to encourage the emergence of strong black congregations and to help support capable pastors, many of whom became leaders in the national church. These congregations often organized community centers providing child care, economic development, and cultural activities as part of their ministries. By the 1960s they were playing a vital role in shaping the Presbyterian Church's engagement in the civil rights movement.

During the 1960s more than 200,000 Puerto Ricans immigrated to New York City. There had been a strong Presbyterian missionary presence in Puerto Rico where a number of congregations had been organized. In the 1950s those congregations in Puerto Rico were received as members of New York City Presbytery. Many Puerto Rican immigrants organized new congregations in New York City,

Another wave of Hispanic immigrants came to the United States from Cuba in the late 1950s and 1960s after the revolution led by Fidel Castro. A number of Cuban pastors who had left Cuba came to New York City where many of them became pastors of Puerto Rican congregations.

During and after the Korean War a large number of Koreans arrived in New York and other U.S. cities. As a result of more than a hundred years of Presbyterian mission presence in Korea, many of the newly arrived immigrants were Presbyterian. They soon organized themselves into congregations that affiliated with local presbyteries.

After World War II, many predominantly white congregations left urban centers to follow their members to burgeoning suburban communities. Establishing new congregations in areas of suburban population growth became a mission priority in the 1950s. Presbyterians concerned about this social trend adopted a policy paper in the late 1950s calling on Presbyterians not to abandon the inner city. That policy, adopted by the General Assembly, asked presbyteries not to approve the sale of property of those congregations choosing to leave their historic urban setting for the suburbs. Instead, the property and resources were to remain in the city to provide ministry to the new residents around the church, with the expectation that congregations should strive to reflect the multicultural mix of people in those changing communities.

There was much theological ferment in the postwar years bolstering the churches' engagement with the urbanization and industrialization that characterized mid-20th century America. H. Richard Niebuhr, in his landmark book, *Christ and Culture,* articulated his own understanding of the role of the church in the world as "being the instrument of Christ transforming society." The way the church performed this role was changing in the 20$^{th}$ century. For many decades, stretching back to the 18$^{th}$ century, the church contributed to the public life of the nation by creating institutions that cared for the well-being of individuals. The establishment of schools, hospitals, clinics, and community centers were ways the church responded to human need. Over time, there emerged foundations and private non-church charitable organizations which provided many of these social services. In the Depression era, this moral vision of a good society helped shape national policy for fuller governmental support of education, health care, and social programs. The churches helped influence and shape public opinion and the ethical commitment of emerging public and private policies and programs. As society began more actively to provide those services to more and more citizens, many churches moved away from direct provision of social services, especially hospitals and schools.

The Civil Rights Movement, the War on Poverty, and the women's movement during the 1960s marked another time of rapid social reform. The churches played a prophetic role, alongside people with limited voice in the political process, pushing for expansion of public and private health, education, and welfare programs. The churches assumed more active roles in holding society accountable to provide and support programs for "the common good." This movement, from works of direct service and charity to a justice agenda of solidarity with people suffering inequity and struggling to gain power to shape their own futures, was significant and not without turmoil. The direction the Board of National Missions took in the 1960s is best understood in this social context.

When I came to work for the Board of National Missions in 1963, Kenneth Neigh had recently become its executive director. He came from Detroit where he had served as Executive Presbyter. He undertook to decentralize the work of the Board of National Missions and aimed to enlarge the responsibility of local church governing bodies in defining and administering the mission of the church in their own localities. Coming from the experience of working with churches in a large city, he argued that each presbytery should craft the mission for its own territory. The role of the Board of National Missions was to support, encourage and provide resources for each presbytery to define and carry out the mission of the Presbyterian Church within its own bounds. At the time Neigh came as executive, the Board of National Missions employed some 1200 "national missionaries" who were employees directly funded by and accountable to the national offices.

This restructure required a transfer of power from the national church to the middle governing bodies. Presbyteries are local bodies of anywhere from 20 to 200 congregations. Synods are regional bodies comprised of several presbyteries. Money that previously directly supported the national church programs was re-allocated to presbyteries and synods according to a formula related to size, population, needs of the region as well as to church membership of each presbytery. These significant changes challenged each presbytery to see not only its congregations, but also the justice and social service ministries of settlement houses, health clinics, and social justice projects more clearly as part of their responsibility, and to understand the presbytery itself as an instrument of mission.

Prior to this re-organization, presbyteries typically had small staffs. During the ten years I worked in East Harlem, the Presbytery of New York City's staff was one part-time Executive Presbyter and an administrative assistant. That pattern was typical of presbyteries across the country. Following this period of reorganization, presbytery staff grew to include locally based specialists in such areas as urban ministry, rural ministry, women's concerns, and Christian education, as well as congregational development. It was not unusual for a presbytery to have a staff of five or more people. Support for these staff people was funded by allocations from the national church to enable a presbytery to design and administer the mission in its own place.

The office of Urban and Industrial Ministries I staffed was caught up in implementing this new national mission strategy. Many inner city congregations and community centers which had been receiving funds from the national church offices were now lodged within the presbytery framework. National assistance for these programs now had to be negotiated between each particular ministry and the presbytery.

The implementation of this national mission strategy guided the tasks and priorities pursued by the Urban and Industrial Ministries Office over the next ten years of my tenure:

**1) Developing an urban cadre across the country.** During my first months on the job, a meeting of inner city clergy from large cities all across the United States was convened. Urban specialist presbytery staff people, as well as inner city pastors, often trained in urban planning, social work, or community organizing, were included in that gathering. This cadre of urban clergy met two or three times a year, sharing experiences across metropolitan and regional lines and helping shape national policy and programs. More than 200 people were involved over the next decade. For many, the encouragement, inspiration, and insight they received from meeting with peers at these gatherings were, in the words of one colleague, "our church." This was especially true when violence wracked urban areas and colleagues supported and counseled each other in the midst of the turbulence.

Worship and Bible study were an important part of these meetings. Preparation for worship regularly involved studying the day's local newspaper, choosing stories for inclusion in prayers of confession, thanksgiving, and intercession. Scriptures for the day were examined for ways they might illuminate the headlines. A songbook with urban ministry themes was compiled for worship.

This rich sharing and collective reflection of colleagues about their urban contexts made its way back to the participants' local congregations and presbyteries. These practitioners, along with their local urban mission committees, developed reports and proposals that came to the floor of local presbytery meetings on issues of poverty, race, housing, public education, jobs, and public safety. Lively debate would ensue and often led to action by presbyteries.

**2) Formulating policy for adoption by General Assembly, including a manual: "Guidelines for Development of Strategy for Metropolitan Mission."** The 1967 General Assembly adopted guidelines for metropolitan mission. Those recommendations were developed over a two-year period with the participation of several hundred metropolitan presbytery executives, inner city pastors, lay leaders from urban congregations, and Presbyterians with experience in community organization, urban planning, and other fields of urban studies and practice. These policies and guidelines encouraged presbyteries to:

- Become familiar with the geography of their cities, including exploring the abilities of the people and of potential financial sources which might be cultivated for support;
- Identify non-geographical communities, not defined by neighborhoods, but by people engaged in common work – educators, health care professionals, government workers, artists; who have mutual interests and commitment such as peace and social justice; people with mutual needs – the handicapped, homeless, unemployed, specific age groups – youth, senior citizens. Are there any of these groups with which members of the congregation are involved? Are there ways to reach out and minister to these communities?
- Identify power structures and decision-making dynamics of the city. Who has power to make decisions in the city and how? Where is power wielded – government, business, labor unions, the press? What groups are left out of decision-making? Where is the church present at these points of power? How can the church support its own members who function in these power structures? Can the church itself exercise influence in the decisions-making processes

of the city? How can the church find ways to enable people with limited power to participate in shaping their own lives, neighborhoods, and cities?

- Become familiar with areas of particular need, suffering, and injustice in the city. Are there ways that the church can stand with and serve those who are suffering? In what ways can the church be in solidarity with people in difficult circumstances? What actions can the church take to bring healing, health and justice to those in need?

**3) Building an Ecumenical Approach to Urban Ministry.** The Metropolitan Strategy statement affirms commitment to ecumenical approaches. In a number of cities, new interchurch and interfaith structures emerged alongside existing councils of churches to facilitate local ecumenical action, such as the Rochester Urban Ministry and metropolitan faith-based organizations in Chicago, New York City, and Washington, DC. Nationally the Presbyterian Church, the Episcopal Church, and the United Church of Christ found they were pursuing common agendas in housing, poverty, public education, urban training and community organization. They began to hold concurrent meetings and then established a Joint Strategy and Action Committee (JSAC). Soon ten denominations affiliated with JSAC. Over time, JSAC formed ecumenical task forces for new church development, affordable housing, criminal justice, Christian education, and others. JSAC became an important catalyst and arena for these much needed ecumenical efforts to address large social concerns. Such increased collaboration produced common programs and pooled resources.

**4) Training for Urban Ministry.** The Urban Training Center for Christian Ministry in Chicago (UTC), with sponsorship from ten national church bodies, trained hundreds of seminarians, men and women clergy and lay leaders in urban mission skills. Students who came from a number of confessional backgrounds were exposed to common methodologies that provided "shared formation in urban ministries."

Over a ten-year period, a series of outstanding directors gave leadership: Kim Myers, author of *Light the Dark Streets*, became the Episcopal Bishop of San Francisco; Jim Morton became the Dean of St. John's Cathedral in New York City; George Younger, an experienced inner city pastor, authored important urban ministry books and became the executive for the American Baptist Conference of New Jersey as well as director of Metropolitan Urban Service Training (MUST).

The "Urban Plunge" became one of the best known UTC programs. Participants were sent into the city with $5 in hand and assigned to "survive" for three days. Community organizing was a regular part of the UTC curriculum. A Ford Foundation grant helped subsidize intensive training for African American clergy from across the country. A series of two-month residential courses provided a place for black clergy to gather, learn and strategize together during the week and enabled them to return to their pulpits for the weekend. Jesse Jackson was on the UTC faculty at that time.

Another large training center was the Methodist Urban Service Training Center in New York City. As it became more ecumenical in scope, the name was changed to Metropolitan Urban Service Training (MUST) and was initially located in Harlem. The first director was Randy Nugent, a Methodist clergyman who later became executive for the Methodist Board of Global Ministries. MUST, along with most of the training centers, was guided by an action-reflection pedagogy. Instead of classrooms, learning took place in congregations, church agencies, community organizations, and government agencies where they worked on issues first-hand. Participants learned skills in urban politics, economics, and community analysis applicable to issues such as housing, public education, poverty, and crime.

The second director of MUST was Bill Webber, a colleague from the East Harlem Protestant Parish. Soon MUST relocated to the campus of New York Theological Seminary where Bill Webber became president. Under his leadership this 100-year-old traditional seminary was transformed into a unique learning center among seminaries. Its curriculum focused on urban ministry, providing hands-on training for clergy from mainline, evangelical, and historical African-American denominations. One of its strengths was its active commitment to provide theological education for practicing clergy who were not seminary graduates, but were already serving congregations.

During this period a number of theological seminaries also began to include course work on urban ministry in their curricula and to provide urban ministry field experiences for their students. In Washington, DC, an ecumenical seminary called InterMet was started with a curriculum built around practical involvement of students in a variety of urban ministries. McCormick Theological Seminary in Chicago, influenced by the work of PIIR and Marshall Scott's leadership, found increased enrollment in its program offering a joint graduate degree in theology and social work.

Each year my office offered graduating seminarians the opportunity to serve in a one-year internship with outstanding experienced inner city pastors. Most of the graduates of that post-seminary internship program went on to years of service in urban Presbyterian and ecumenical congregations and projects.

**5) Congregation-based Community Organizing (CBCO).** The modern community organization movement traces its beginnings to Saul Alinsky's groundbreaking work in the Back of the Yards neighborhood of Chicago in the 1930s. He brilliantly brought the institutional power of churches, unions, schools, and charitable organizations together to challenge the meat-packing industry to improve the living conditions in the neighborhood the companies largely controlled. Community organizing, rooted in neighborhood-based institutions, proved to be an effective strategy for enabling grassroots democracy, training leaders to be effective in public life, and building power to help families and communities to survive and thrive.

The first week on the job, I attended a Presbytery of Chicago consultation on community organizations with local pastors engaged in organizing. Saul Alinsky himself led that consultation. I had first read his book,

*Reveille for Radicals*, in college in 1947. I had used some of his tactics in East Harlem and in my teaching of urban industrial courses in Taiwan. He was pleased when I told him about translating his book into Chinese. We became friends and colleagues over the next nine years until his death in 1972. From him I learned political toughness, humor in the midst of conflict, and how important it is to find and train good leaders in any endeavor.

There were three active organizing groups in Chicago staffed by the Industrial Areas Foundation (IAF), the umbrella organization Alinsky created. They were The Woodlawn Organization (TWO) just south of the University of Chicago, the Northwest Community Organization (NTO), and the Pilsen Neighborhood Organization. Presbyterians were active in the starting of TWO. David Ramage was the urban ministry staff person in the Chicago Presbytery at that time. Charles Leber and Buck Blakely, co-pastors of First Presbyterian Church in Woodlawn, were a dynamic bi-racial team committed to strengthening their impoverished neighborhood. To admiring friends this tandem was known as "Buck and Chuck."

Community organizing has proven to be an effective strategy in moving beyond social service models toward helping build organizations enabling neighborhoods to gain power for themselves. In the way that the Presbyterian Church has been a pioneer in urban ministry, helping to develop education, health and social services in American cities, the Presbyterian Church also became a leader in the growing movement of faith-based community organizing. To people lacking power to participate in decisions affecting their lives, community organizing brought skills for building an organization of organizations – churches, unions, businesses, schools, and non-profits – where the values of those communities were carried into public life. CBCOs are non-partisan, but engage themselves in political issues. Organization leaders hold hundreds of one-on-one meetings enlisting participation and encouraging citizens to address issues they feel most deeply about. The next steps are house meetings and research actions where people's most pressing concerns are discussed and plans are generated for action.

Community organizing is also an effective tool for allowing people of different faith traditions, races, and income levels to come together around issues that affect them all. In the process they find common ground, overcoming barriers as they act together When community organizing is done well, it provides the arena for people to tell their stories in public, to name their pain and anger, to articulate a course of effective action and to hold those in positions of power accountable to the interests of the people.

In many ways, community organizing keeps the church grounded in the reality of those experiencing poverty and holds congregations accountable. The Guidelines for Development of Strategy for Metropolitan Mission, the urban policy of the Presbyterian Church adopted in 1967, puts it this way: "Many Christians understand the limitations that their own isolation from the 'culture of poverty' places on their ability to understand 'what is good for the poor.' Community organization enables persons alienated from an affluent culture to speak out and be heard across social, economic and cultural barriers. Christians and others hearing and responding to these voices who are enabled to speak by community organization, are served by a sorely needed check on the self-centeredness and sin which Christians should know infects all their well-meaning and charitable actions."

Some critics view community organizing as too controversial or too adversarial. Some church people become anxious whenever there is talk of power, fearful that it may be corrupting. Alinsky argued that tension between power holders is the only thing that will bring about change, making conflict inherent in community organizing. He defined power, in its purest form, as "the ability to accomplish things."

In the urban offices of the denominations there were strong differences about the efficacy of community organizing. I remember being at an ecumenical meeting when one of my peers turned to me and said, "What you Presbyterians are doing when you support community organizing is pouring poison into the well of ecumenicity." I disagreed. Biblical prophets knew very well there would be tension when they advocated for

God's justice. Power appears in the scriptures as an attribute of God and a gift given to humanity. In addition, the scripture gives guidance on the use and limits of power.

Mike Miller, a veteran organizer, wrote in his book, *A Community Organizer's Tale,* about how in the debate about the church supporting community organizing, the Protestant journal, *Christian Century,* opposed Alinsky's tactics and conservative Catholic journals labeled him a Communist and agitator. Another major Protestant journal, *Christianity and Crisis,* as well as the *National Catholic Reporter,* supported Alinsky and the churches' involvement.

As I observed the impact of dozens of community organizations, with hundreds of congregations involved, and their success in empowering change in their communities, I became convinced that CBCO was a critically important strategy for urban ministry. This was no longer experimental, but a proven and effective methodology for social change and congregational revitalization. I was interested, beyond getting local churches involved, to see training of clergy and laity in the methodologies of community organizing. There are practices in community organizing that strengthen local congregations, such as leadership development, building a strong relational culture, and effectiveness in carrying the church's concerns into public life. Many churches saw The Woodlawn Organization's effectiveness, and the vitality of First Presbyterian Church, Chicago, and said, "We want this for our place, too." Congregation-based community organizing increasingly became a priority in the work of the Urban Ministry offices of several denominations.

At that time, IAF did not have its formal training program in place. The office provided opportunities for people to meet with Alinsky for training and formation. For several years, our office sponsored national conferences at the YMCA conference center in Asilomar, California. These were ten-day training sessions for twenty to forty ministers, not aimed at training organizers, but rather familiarizing clergy with the methods and practices of organizing and how it might happen in their settings. Training for community organizing was part of the curriculum at the

Urban Training Center. In Chicago. Saul Alinsky gave lectures at Union Theological Seminary and also met with leaders of a number of denominations to discuss the relevance of organizing for the social agendas of their congregations.

National church urban offices also supported those who wanted to consider community organizing as a vocation. The training of an organizer entailed a year's probationary tenure in Chicago, working with one of the Chicago organizations with Alinsky providing oversight and support. If they passed that milestone, they worked for another year as an organizer in a different organization under the supervision of a senior organizer. After two years, the trainee might be considered a "professional organizer." Finding enough skilled organizers has always been one of the greatest challenges in the community organizing movement.

Organizing efforts started in Rochester, San Francisco, Minneapolis, Buffalo, New York and other cities. The FIGHT (For Integration, God, and Housing Today) organization in Rochester brokered a hard-earned victory against the Kodak Corporation over their hiring practices with respect to the African-American work force. After Kodak's top executives undermined negotiated concessions, the FIGHT organization enlisted the proxy votes of church bodies which owned Kodak stock and brought their grievances to an annual stockholders' meeting. The tactic was successful and showed the effectiveness of demands for corporate responsibility by stockholders.

Following this experience, a number of denominations, Roman Catholic orders, national mission agencies and other ethical investors formed the Interfaith Center for Corporate Responsibility (ICCR). Today, some 350 religious organizations, denominations, congregations, and religious orders participate in the work of ICCR. Community organizing maintains that one significant form of power is "organized money." ICCR examines corporations in which their members hold shares. They screen business practices for product quality; fair treatment of employees; arms industry involvement; guns, alcohol, and tobacco production; environmental concerns; production practices in their overseas operations; and other ethical issues. The ICCR members use their shareholder voting power to address concerns with company leadership and the other shareholders. ICCR provides education to churches and religious bodies about the policies and practices of the corporations in which they hold stock.

After Alinsky's death in 1972 the leadership of IAF formalized its training efforts for organizers. The 1980s saw a number of new organizations emerge in Texas and the Southwest, as well as the reviving of organizations in Midwest and East Coast cities. At present, IAF organizers staff more than 60 organizations. There are three other major national networks – PICO, DART, and the Gamaliel Foundation – and several smaller regional networks. Several hundred professional organizers work with more than 175 CBCOs around the country in small towns as well as in cities. The most recent study by Interfaith Funders counts over 4,000 synagogues and churches as members.

Community organization has gotten additional press coverage in recent years, as President Barack Obama worked for three years as a community organizer in Chicago before he entered politics. In her senior year at Wellesley College, Hillary Clinton did major research and wrote a paper about Saul Alinsky and the Industrial Areas Foundation. During recent years the CBCO movement has attracted the attention of academics. Some of their published studies provide stories and analysis of effective organizations, including reports on the role of the churches. There have now appeared a number of books written by seasoned organizers telling the stories of their organizations. Many are seeing community organizing to be an important strategy for reinvigorating democracy as citizens experience the capacity to act powerfully in their own interests.

In an ecumenical effort to broaden support for community organizing, several denominations joined in forming the Interfaith Foundation for Community Organizing (IFCO). Initially, this ecumenical foundation provided a way to pool the monies of the individual denominations and each was represented on the board. Soon, IFCO began to focus on training of African-American organizers and eventually moved into issues of international racial justice. Years later, denominations and funders interested in community organizing created Interfaith Funders to research the field and advocate for funding from the larger foundation community.

**6) Additional Organizing Efforts and Social Justice Campaigns.** This decade was a troubled time in American history. The office tried to support and resource a variety of efforts of churches, presbyteries, and social movements across the country as they arose. The National Council of Churches' Migrant Ministry for over 30 years had been working to serve the needs of migrant farm workers who were the lowest paid and suffered harder conditions than almost any other group of American laborers. In the 1950s and 1960s the churches' migrant ministry played an active role in raising consciousness among the churches to support the work of Cesar Chavez in organizing the National Farm Workers Union. Church members in many cities participated actively in organizing boycotts of grapes and other crops picked by exploited immigrant farm laborers. These national boycotts helped to bring pressure on growers to improve working conditions and pay for migrant harvesters and were successful in bringing about legislation in several states for more humane and just conditions.

With leaders like Chris Hartmire, who later joined the National Farm Workers Union staff, the churches have been at the forefront in organizing consumer pressure through boycotts to influence corporation policies. The Presbyterian Church has been active in a number of boycotts and campaigns since, including the Taco Bell boycott, J. P. Stevens, and recently tomato growers' wage campaigns in Florida. When many manufacturing plants in older industrial cities downsized or closed or moved their production to plants overseas, the churches were active in ministering to displaced workers and in negotiating for more humane programs for transition on behalf of those losing their jobs.

During the 1950s and 1960s teams of clergy established Industrial Missions in a number of cities, particularly with help from the United Church of Christ, the Episcopal Church, and Presbyterian and Methodist Churches. The first team began its work in Detroit. During the next two decades such teams came into being in a dozen other industrial cities, as well as abroad. Some urban missioners worked with industrial laborers in factories. Others worked to create significant interaction between workers, unions and management. Still others served as industrial chaplains. They helped pioneer the field of organizational development, helping companies create more humane conditions in the workplace and pressing for more active participation of workers in decision making.

My seminary roommate, Bob Batchelder, involved earlier in a PIIR *Students-in-Industry* project, became a member of the Detroit Industrial Mission. In a book about his experience he writes an interesting chapter on building contractors who were wrestling with the ethical dilemma of widespread collusion in the industry around bidding practices. They acknowledged the uneasiness they felt about this practice, but they also understood the pressures and need to remain competitive. Their deliberations led to the establishment of an ethics committee in Detroit's Council of Building Trades and a Code of Ethics Covenant that members of the association adopted. This story tells how the church might provide a space for Christians to self-consciously look at their occupations and dilemmas and find ways to act more responsibly and ethically. In the light of the ascendancy of the financial sector of American life and its inherent practices that maximize profit at all costs, such work seems more needed than ever.

In the 1960s, as the struggle for racial justice came to the fore and uprisings occurred in Detroit and other major cities across the country, the industrial missions found themselves called to assist in mediating. They were acknowledged to have built relationships of trust on all sides of these struggles. They had built relationships with labor unions and labor leaders and also with Black power leaders and groups. They were also trusted by management, and so could at times play a constructive role in getting across to police, city government, and management what some of these communities were saying. They created the tables where it was possible to negotiate communications and agreements that helped bring an end to open rioting and also enabled the city leaders to respond to some of the principal grievances.

During the 1970s, industrial mission in Detroit began working with both labor and management on issues of race. They produced one of the first documents in the 1960s that very clearly articulated for the white churches and white management that uprisings and riots were not about social disorder in the black community, as much as about social inequities and racism of the dominant culture. They brought people together to begin to acknowledge these realities and to be willing to move, though slowly, toward changes.

In 1996 ecumenical labor work found a new voice with the forming of Interfaith Worker Justice (IWJ). This table enabled Protestants, Catholics, Jews, Muslims, and Buddhists along with labor members and others to actively intervene in dozens of labor disputes. They have organized IWJ chapters in many states and cities and trained a number of mostly young people to staff these new organizations. For instance, they have been effective in helping workers organize unions in sectors such as the hotel and hospitality industry.

In a more rural setting, the Mountaineer Mining Mission (MMM) had for many years served mine workers in small towns in Kentucky and West Virginia. The United Mine Workers Union (UMW) owned several hospitals built with union dues that provided much needed quality medical care. In the mid-1960s, when operating losses for the hospitals were mounting, the UMW made a decision to close those facilities. The miners and their families and the local communities were distressed with the union action. The MMM approached the Board of National Missions to take over the management of the hospitals rather than have them closed and see people suffer. Members of our staff resourced those hospitals through a transition to private ownership and management which included roles for the union locals in ongoing administration of those hospitals. This forgotten part of the Presbyterian Church's history of engagement with labor was a shining accomplishment of the Board of National Missions during Kenneth Neigh's administration (1960-72).

Another success was the Child Development Group of Mississippi (CDGM). Under President Johnson's War on Poverty, projects were generally administered by state governments. There was a provision that allowed special demonstration projects to be administered through colleges and universities. CDGM, a state-wide program and forerunner of the Head Start Program for Early Childhood Education, was established in Mississippi as a War on Poverty program. It was administered through Mary Holmes College, a Board of National Missions owned and operated junior college in Mississippi. Marian Wright Edelman, later founder and director of Children's Defense Fund, helped with that effort. The parents associations that were organized at many of the Head Start locations succeeded in playing a leading role in the development of the Mississippi Freedom Democratic Party which nominated delegates to be seated at the 1968 Democratic Convention.

Sargent Shriver was Johnson's administrator for the War on Poverty at that time. Pressure from southern Congressmen was exerted on him to cut funding for CDGM. This was happening when the first joint national meeting of urban specialists from the United Church of Christ, the Episcopal Church and Presbyterian churches was scheduled. We moved our meeting from Chicago to Washington and picketed Sargent Shriver's office. Several of us met with him to urge continued funding. Full page ads in the New York Times and several other newspapers around the country called for the preservation of these Mississippi programs. Shriver agreed to continue support and persuaded Johnson to back him up over the objections of the Mississippi Congressmen.

**7) Broad-based Public Policy.** With the founding of the Joint Strategy and Action Committee (JSAC), denominational staff found we could be more effective by collaborating with each other on matters of public policy. By the mid-1960s the Episcopal, United Church of Christ and Presbyterian leaders began to hold concurrent and joint meetings. JSAC was successful in bringing into being the Interreligious Foundation for Community Organization (IFCO) and the Interfaith Center for Corporate Responsibility (ICCR).

Three of the concerns we worked on together were affordable housing, public education and national political action. In the area of affordable housing there was a groundswell coming from the local level to the national level. Many congregations were involved in sponsoring low-income housing, creating tenants' rights groups, pressuring banks to end redlining practices, monitoring discriminatory real estate practices, and more. The religious organizations sponsored more Housing and Urban Development Department (HUD) subsidized housing in the 1960s for senior citizens than all other sponsors. The director of the HUD's senior citizens housing department was a Presbyterian minister who had been one of our post-seminary urban interns. As these issues came to our awareness from the local level we compared notes and decided to address these same issues at the national level. Several denominations, along with secular groups, banded together to form the National Low Income Housing Coalition which now has many sponsors along with the churches. The Board of National Missions of the Presbyterian Church added a full-time staff person, Robert Johnson, to assist presbyteries and congregations with housing ministries.

At the local level, congregations were also working diligently to assure that there was adequate funding for public education for teachers and facilities. Churches lobbied school boards for increased allocations to failing schools. They set up tutoring and study centers to assist the students in the classroom. Several denominations collaborated to create a National Ministry for Public Education. They lobbied for larger allocations of federal dollars for public education across the country and for innovative ways to enhance the skills of teachers and the success of students.

Many other urban issues called for public policy initiatives at the national level. In 1970 an organization named IMPACT was created whose mission was to keep congregations informed on key legislation before Congress and to be a lobbying arm for domestic issues that churches believed were important. While most denominational Washington offices lobbied Congress on the basis of policy positions of their church bodies, IMPACT kept track of key legislation and mobilized hundreds of congregations and their members to advocate when key legislation came before Congress. IMPACT also organized a number of state chapters which functioned in relation to state government as well as to national government.

**8) International Dimensions of Urban Industrial Mission.** The Board of National Missions worked on joint ventures with the Overseas Mission Board, known then as the Commission on Ecumenical Mission and Relations (COEMAR). As rapid urbanization and industrialization were changing Asian, African, and Latin American countries, there was increasing conversation between the domestic programs of the Presbyterian Church USA and their international mission activities. These discussions brought about funding for such initiatives. The domestic and the overseas mission boards together established a joint Office for Urban and Industrial Mission. Churches to which we had long been related overseas were looking for ways to be effective in times of rapid social change and social dislocation. We began to increase support of people from churches abroad to have training opportunities in the USA and other countries, enriching both American churches and international trainees through exchange of experience.

As our office provided grant support to innovative efforts around the world, I was able to travel to a number of countries where we had mission partner churches to consult with them about the situations and opportunities. In the USA, our office participated with other American churches to found the North American Congress on Latin America (NACLA) and the Middle East Research and Information Project (MERIP). COEMAR was adjusting its international agenda toward reducing the number of its American missionaries, releasing substantial resources for block grants to overseas missions that had become autonomous churches in the postwar period.

By virtue of my role in the Presbyterian Church, I was invited in 1966 to sit on the new World Council of Churches Advisory Committee for Urban Industrial Mission. The WCC was receiving requests from member churches in Asia, Africa, and Latin America for help in finding significant ways to respond to urbanization and industrialization in those regions.

**9) Support for Emerging Local Ministry Initiatives.** In the United States, the UIM office found itself engaged in helping presbyteries initiate new projects in many cities. The Urban Office worked with local congregations and agencies across the country seeking to respond to challenges in their contexts in experimental and creative ways. There were a number of efforts reaching out to low-income public housing projects and high-rise apartment buildings. Shopping center ministries and coffee house ministries proliferated, providing settings for music, social discourse, and building community. There were innovative programs for youth and seniors.

In the Los Angeles Regional Goals Project several denominations pooled resources to support a full-time clergy-person who became part of the Greater Los Angeles Urban Planning Office. A Presbyterian lay leader, Calvin Hamilton, was the urban planner who headed that office. Forty congregations in that city became "Centers of Choice" where people gathered to explore how interests, values and aspirations of citizens could shape the city's physical development.

An ecumenical ministry initiated by American Baptists in Philadelphia sought to form congregations drawn from communities of people engaged in common vocations such as health care professionals, lawyers, and government workers. They met to explore how their faith was lived out in their work and how their faith might influence their secular vocations.

All these efforts demonstrate the role the national church might have in providing seed money and encouragement for experimentation at the local level. A number of these efforts were understandably controversial, given the volatile nature of the times. In the early 1970s there was a major restructuring of the Presbyterian national offices, not so much in creative response to the changes that had taken place in the society and churches since the 1960s, but instead in defensive reaction resisting those changes. During the previous decade the Board of National Missions Division of Church Strategy and Development was comprised of some twelve departments. There were separate offices for Christian Education, Higher

Education, Community Organization, Health Ministries, Development of New Congregations, Rural Ministries, Women's Concerns, Research and Planning and more, as well as the Urban Industrial Ministry office. I imagined a new structure working more coherently if all the offices saw their work within an overarching urban and industrial ministry umbrella. Understandably each of these offices was interested in continuing under the new structure. When the dust settled from the restructuring, the Urban Industrial Office no longer had any box on the organizational chart. Far from becoming an overall perspective, the urban office simply disappeared.

The restructuring that took place, some would argue, was a reaction to a "radical" agenda enacted by a national staff out of touch with the church and not accountable to the membership for its actions. From my perspective, we were paying very close attention to the needs of clergy and laity in local, urban congregations rather than attempting to consolidate power at the national level. Careful effort was made to empower local congregations and governing bodies in allocating responsibility and resources to empower them. In a chapter I wrote about the history of urban ministry in the book, *Churches, Cities and Human Community: Urban Ministry in the United States 1945-1985*, I concluded, "It is possible to document that the 1960s represented the fullest expression and implementation of Presbyterian participatory and representational policy and accountability to be seen in this century. By the early 1970s the political turning away from American commitment to government initiatives in addressing major critical social issues in housing, education, health and poverty was accompanied by a drawing back by the Presbyterian Church."

The Presbyterian Church had a prolonged period when there was no urban office. The urban agenda did not go away but much of the national urban ministry leadership, with its skills and experience, was dispersed. In the 1980s, Philip Newell and Pat Roach provided new national leadership. After a move of the national church offices to Louisville, Kentucky, Phil Tom and Trey Hammond served as staff for the urban office. New urban mission policy recommendations were adopted by the General Assembly in its 1995 report entitled, *Urban Ministry Until the Year 2005.*

Following that restructure, with my office closed, I applied for some of the newly defined positions, but was not hired. It was clear that my time on the Presbyterian Church national staff was over. As I was beginning to cast around for a new job, Emilio Castro, the Secretary for Evangelism in the World Council of Churches approached me about coming to be director of the WCC Urban Industrial Mission office in Geneva. I was familiar with the work of the office, having been part of the UIM advisory committee since the office was established in 1965.

Emilio took Kathy and me to dinner and by the end of the meal we were convinced that this was to be the next chapter of our lives. We thought it would be a great opportunity for our four boys to experience another country and to be exposed to an international environment. We sold our house, packed up our belongings and headed for Geneva in September of 1972.

—— ⚬ ——

# CHAPTER 5

# **A Global Desk:** The World Council of Churches in Geneva (1972-1981)

AT THE PRESBYTERIAN Urban and Industrial Mission desk at the Interchurch Center in New York, I had become involved with the World Council of Church's Urban and Industrial Mission (UIM) program. The UIM office was first proposed in 1964 when delegates from Asia and Africa who were in New Delhi at the Fourth WCC Assembly advocated that WCC should take initiative to help the churches respond to the rapid social changes they were experiencing because of industrialization and urbanization. In 1965, the WCC established an Urban Industrial Mission office as part of the WCC's Commission on World Mission and Evangelism.

From its beginning, the World Council of Church's programs primarily took the shape of regional and international conferences along with major studies on such subjects as Rapid Social Change and Eucharist, Baptism, and Ministry. As the UIM office was taking shape in 1965 a different pattern emerged. Instead of generating internationally conceived programs, WCC leadership set out to identify local people and places where significant church response to urbanization and industrialization was already taking place. Prior to my coming to the office, regional offices and contact groups had been established in Asia (Hong Kong), Africa (Nairobi), Latin America (Mexico City), and Europe (Amsterdam). Instead of developing a WCC UIM "program," the job of the WCC office entailed identifying initiatives already underway and assisting regional and national efforts to enhance communication and support among such people and programs.

A premise of UIM's work was, "If there is something God wants to have happening, there is a good possibility it is happening." This conviction had already proven true in the ten years of the UIM's work prior to my arrival. It was exciting and inspiring to discover that God's spirit had called men and women to vocations in a great variety of responses to the realities of urbanization and industrialization. We could already identify 500 projects on-going in over 60 countries. The job of the office, in addition to discovering where such activity was happening, was to help these projects discover each other, to learn from and to inspire one another. Within a few years, a worldwide sense of solidarity and mutual engagement in a common ministry came into being. Those leaders working at the grassroots level, reflecting together on how the World Council could best support them and their efforts, articulated eight priorities for WCC's UIM work. Here are some examples of the ways these priorities were implemented:

## 1) Support local initiatives and concrete local involvements in Urban and Industrial Mission

As the regional contact offices and groups in Asia, Africa, Latin American, Europe, and North America became operational, they identified many additional programs in their regions. At their meetings, representatives in the churches from each country gave compelling national reports. These reports described the activities of how congregations and church agencies were working with and serving people in cities. These national and regional reports were circulated among all the regions. Each region then also proposed to WCC the particular programs which could be strengthened by support from the member churches of WCC. An international WCC UIM contact group representing all the regions then produced a list with descriptions of the needs which it circulated to member churches. Such worldwide ecumenical support furthered remarkable local initiatives taking place all around the world.

In Mumbai (formerly Bombay) India, there were several programs in large squatter communities. The Janata Colony, with a population of

70,000, was spread over 54 acres of land. Most of the residents had been moved there 20 years earlier from another slum area when urban renewal efforts had destroyed their housing. Adjacent to Janata, a national atomic research center was being constructed. The squatter land was annexed to build housing and recreational facilities for the center's workforce. The Supreme Court rejected an appeal by the Janata residents to halt demolition of their community.

For years, the churches of Bombay had assisted Janata squatter residents by starting schools, clinics, and forming new congregations. When the community came to feel it was under siege, the UIM-connected agencies helped organize the Bombay Urban Industrial League for Development (BUILD). A march of 50,000 interested people and a hunger strike were undertaken to call awareness to the plight. They were not able to deter the eviction. When police came to remove the residents, local church leaders stood with the community. Power lines were cut and bulldozers started to level housing. The residents were forced to move to an alternative site two miles away, which was swampy and not as suitable a habitat, and rebuild with what they were able to salvage from their old homes. In the new location, BUILD helped in resettlement. New schools and clinics were initiated and helped foster a new sense of community. With continuing pressure from churches and agencies, the government began to allocate some resources to enhance the quality of life in the community.

One church group partnered with textile workers in Seoul, South Korea. A *Students-in-Industry* project in the 1960s had provided seminarians an opportunity to see firsthand the working conditions in factories. Many of these interns went on to serve churches and agencies that related to the needs of people working in factories. In the 1970s there was a huge influx of young women from rural communities into the cities where many were employed at textile factories, earning less than half of the wages of men, and often terribly mistreated in the workplace. A pastor, Rev. Cho Hwa Soon, undertook a ministry with women workers living in a textile plant compound of worker housing. She found places for the women to gather for regular meetings and study, helped support union organization activities, and encouraged worker advocacy in the plant. These efforts were viewed by the government as subversive. Many arrests were made of workers in UIM programs. A number of them experienced torture during their incarceration.

In 1978, at the Dong-Il Textile Company in the port of Inchon, a combustible situation ignited. The workforce was 85% women and they were successful, with support from UIM partner agencies and churches, in forming a union that had women in leadership roles. Disgruntled men workers, along with support of the management, and outside forces interested in dismantling the union, used the occasion of the annual union election to raid the union office, smash the ballot boxes, and beat and humiliate the women union leaders, smearing them with excrement. The company fired the women workers rather than the perpetrators of the raid. The women workers met in church buildings and offices. Hunger strikes were organized and attention was called to this workplace injustice in the press around the world. Finally, the company agreed to re-hire them, but when they came back to work, the company required them to sign a document admitting their fault in the uproar and agreeing that they would not cause the company any more trouble. The 126 who refused to sign were once again fired. These workers were blacklisted and had trouble getting jobs elsewhere.

The women came to a meeting at the Christian Building in Seoul and their plight was the focus of a Friday night prayer meeting. During the worship 400 plain-clothes police descended on the service, beat up protesters, including prominent church leaders, and arrested dozens of the women workers. The Women's Worker Fellowship supported the women in prison and continues to advocate for women workers to this day.

In 1979, another plant situated in South Korea exploded in violence directed at workers. The YH Trading Company suddenly closed its doors and left its workforce unemployed and homeless, as many of them lived in factory housing. A group of female workers had initially staged a sit-in at the plant after the closing, but they were removed by the police. They then appealed to the National Democratic Party (NDP), which stood in opposition to the repressive government of President Park Chung Hee, and were granted use of the party's office building for protest and as a place to sleep. At 2 AM, over a thousand police officers entered the headquarters in riot gear and violently beat workers, reporters, and leaders of the NDP, including two assemblymen. One young woman died in the raid and 172 workers were arrested, along with 26 NDP members. Though the workers were soon released and promised jobs, actually most of them were put on buses and returned to their rural communities. The government used this occasion to crack down on UIM allies, charging that UIM masterminded the protests. The government controlled press featured such headlines as "Church Group Incites Labor Feud" and "A Sinister Force Hell-bent on Building Socialist State."

This excessive use of violence by the government to quell protest and the arrests and torture of activists and opposition politicians contributed to the collapse of the Park regime. All the opposition legislators resigned in protest and thousands filled the streets in the largest protest movement in Park's 18-year rule. In the upheaval, Park was assassinated and the government was re-constituted. Throughout all this upheaval, the local church-related organizations affiliated with UIM had stood with, advocated for, and suffered with those workers striving for their God-given dignity and rights. Overseas, aware of the injustices in the factories, church groups in the United States brought to the attention of U.S. companies doing business with Korean textile manufacturers the situation of young women in those workplaces.

Most of the projects we funded were similar to the examples above in that they were not directed by the WCC, but were important local experiments in urban-industrial mission which we encouraged and supported. The grants we provided were not large, but demonstrated the solidarity of the world Christian community. Implicit in the grants was a commitment to make their experiences, techniques, and methodologies known throughout the world.

The UIM program expanded rapidly from an initial $50,000 budget by nearly doubling each year during the first six years. The donor churches were increasingly attracted to the UIM style of support and encouragement for local initiatives. Within a few years their financial support for program grants grew to exceed $3 million. By 1972, programs which had received previous grants had learned how to access another $6 million from other WCC designated sources for on-going projects. The grants from the UIM budget were funding new experimental endeavors with less restriction and reporting requirements appropriate to the needs of churches and organizing in developing countries.

**2) Aid in sustaining networks of communication, with the aim to enable communication among localities, rather than to pass information from the center to the periphery.**

Information sharing among groups doing innovative work around the world was clearly an important function the WCC could play with its wide network of relationships. This being prior to computers and the Internet, our primary medium would necessarily be print. In the WCC, UIM contact groups became increasingly aware that local newsletters, reports, and magazine articles describing the work were being published. They explored how such information might be gathered and what might be the best way to share it.

The Chicago-based Presbyterian Institute of Industrial Relations (PIIR) had been collecting such information on the American urban, industrial scene for more than forty years. Marshall Scott, the PIIR director, was open to exploring such a possibility for international efforts. Bobbi Wells-Hargleroad, a journalist and researcher working with national peace movements, was hired and moved to Chicago to join the staff of PIIR in this documentation project. Under her direction, there came into being a monthly newsletter for sharing information.

Before long, information from hundreds of organizations began to flood into that office. The staff would publish three or four full stories and then abstract other communications into a monthly newsletter. The logo of *The Abstract Service* was a tangled web of strings or threads with lots of nodes and nexus points where they crossed each other. The articles were cataloged by country and sometimes by subject. The newsletter was circulated to all the programs in the UIM network and to member churches of the WCC as well as to news agencies.

The information sharing center soon took the name, Institute on the Church in Urban Industrial Society, or ICUIS. Very soon dozens of publications were arriving at ICUIS every week, along with requests for additional information. ICUIS provided the vehicle for stories and actions from the local level to reach a worldwide constituency. ICUIS would gather articles around themes, such as community organizing or corporate responsibility, or around specific country profiles. Its archive, covering 35 years of reports and clippings, is now housed at the library of the University of Illinois, Chicago campus.

In an essay describing the work of ICIUS for a UIM report, Hargleroad saw information sharing as essential, especially as the information shared is not so much about data, but about people, living creatively, faithfully, and sometimes sacrificially in their contexts. By allowing an exchange of stories and ideas, the whole worldwide community was served and local initiatives were strengthened and affirmed as their stories found a wide audience. Sometimes the information ICUIS gathered from grassroots sources, such as an arrest or violent actions taken against a remote squatter village, shed light on what might have been little publicized in the regular press. Such exposure sometimes entirely reversed a situation. Before the instantaneous information of the Internet, it was a vital way for neglected communities to find a voice for articulating and sharing their experience.

By 1970, the Christian Conference of Asia began an effort named Documentation for Action Groups in Asia (DAGA). Local groups from the 17 Asian counties where UIM was active could keep each other informed about particular issues, actions, and concerns. DAGA also did research related to particular political or economic situations local groups were encountering. The DAGA office became a regular stop for correspondents on the Asian beat from European and North American newspapers and magazines.

### 3) Assist in leadership development through training events and providing for training of selected individuals.

In many countries and regions, training for urban mission was identified as a need as churches looked for ways to help people increase their skills. Our office was frequently consulted and invited to partner with such training activities.

The *Students-in-Industry* program became a widely used model providing practical experience with workers, coupled with biblical and theological reflection. The training included exposure to labor union leaders, public officials, and corporation managers. These efforts were taking place in New York, Chicago, and New Haven in the U.S., as well as Canada, Korea, Japan, Taiwan, Brazil, and a number of African countries.

In the 1960s, a number of ecumenical urban training centers had been established in cities across the United States and in Canada. George Younger, in a book which chronicled the growth of this network of training centers, described the methodology of this coalition as "action training," learning by engagement and reflection. The trainers in the centers were a highly skilled cadre, many with experience in inner city ministry and with graduate degrees in urban studies. Many of the trainers shared an interest in global urbanization issues and participated in WCC UIM activities and utilized ecumenical resources. These training institutes often sent American students to training centers in other countries for exposure to different urban contexts and provided learning opportunities for international students studying in Canada and the USA.

In Germany, industries and labor unions approached the churches to utilize Evangelical Academies for training. The academies were chateaus and estates that had been used by the Nazis and were given to the church after the war as conference and training centers. These academies developed regular training programs for young apprentices beginning their careers in industry. They provided an orientation to life in the working world, understanding unions and labor, and ethics in the work place.

In Africa, UIM sponsored four-month residential courses entitled *Training for Urban/Industrial Ministry.* These were held in alternating years in East Africa in English and the next year in West Africa in French. Interns lived in a village for three weeks, exploring the traditions, patterns, and challenges for those in rural settings. In the next three-week stint, as laborers in a factory setting, they met with labor leaders and others familiar with the forces of industrialization. The third setting was exposure to the dynamics of a city, where for three weeks they would immerse themselves in the lives of people living in an urban parish and learn through them about their work and challenges. They were exposed to experts who could help them understand the political and economic life of the city. At the end of their immersion, there followed a time of integrating their learning and exploring how it might help them engage in their situations back home.

WCC UIM was also able to respond to requests from localities to provide opportunities for their leaders to travel abroad, seek training, or even work on graduate degrees in urban studies. One of the joys of the UIM work was meeting talented, committed people from all over the world and exploring ways to open doors for their professional development and exposure to learning opportunities.

Jerome Lee, a young Taiwanese engineer, spent several months at the William Temple Institute and Sheffield Industrial Mission in Britain, the Iona Community in Scotland, the Mission Populaire in France, and finally the Evangelical Academies in Germany with support from UIM. The idea that every vocation was a way to serve God led Lee to create a Bible study group among his engineering peers in Taiwan to explore the ethical implications of their work.

George Matthew from India and Koson Srisang from Thailand did Ph.D. studies in political science at the University of Chicago. George Matthew returned from the University of Chicago to found a training center in New Dehli which has had national impact through community empowerment events, especially with women, and through its influence on national and local legislatures. Srisang returned to become a university chaplain in Bangkok and later served on the WCC staff on international development issues.

Oh Jae Shik, a Student Christian Movement leader and political activist from Korea, after theological study at Yale, spent time with a number of programs in the USA that were engaged in action for social change. He visited the Southern Christian Leadership Conference, where he stayed with Andrew Young and his family, as they participated along with Martin Luther King in demonstrations in Atlanta; he worked with the National Council of Church's Delta Ministry project in Mississippi; he stayed with Caesar Chavez's family in California where he participated in organizing with the United Farm Workers Union; and, finally, he joined a church-sponsored two week community organizing session taught by Saul Alinsky. He went on to join the Christian Conference of Asia's staff for urban industrial mission and serve as a key leader in Asian Committee for People's Organization (ACPO), the community organizing training center for the region.

Sam Kobia of Kenya had been president of the All Africa Student Christian Movement. He was assisted in completing a master's degree in development economics from MIT. His thesis documented community organizing in African cities. He worked at the WCC UIM office and then was the executive of the National Conference of Churches of Kenya. Later he became the General Secretary of the World Council of Churches.

## 4) Encourage and aid churches in efforts to organize people in low income neighborhoods to gain power to change the conditions in which they live and work.

One of the key shifts in thinking in worldwide ecclesial circles in the 1960s was moving from direct service programs to programs of empowerment. Many American churches saw in the community organizing movement, initiated by Saul Alinsky, an effective strategy for shaping public life. Churches funded community organizing efforts and encouraged congregations and leaders to invest in building local organizations. This type of congregational based organizing became a key part of urban mission strategy in many American cities.

In other regions of the world, there was a growing awareness that empowerment of those living in deprived communities could be a genuine part of the church's mission. The Christian Conference of Asia and the Roman Catholic Asian Bishops conference recognized the effectiveness of such church initiated organizing in vital "people power" programs among squatters in South Korea, among fishing people in Hong Kong, factory labor slums in Japan, and squatter communities in India. These church leaders founded the Asian Center for People's Organizations (ACPO) in Manila. Herbert White, a veteran organizer who had done successful organizing and training in several cities in the USA and Asia, came to Manila to give leadership to organizing this center. Over the next 10 years, more than 200 leaders from 14 Asian countries learned professional organizing skills. The strategies and practices of the congregation-based community organizing movement in the U.S. were studied and adapted by ACPO to the various contexts throughout Asia. The ACPO trainers chose Tondo, one of the largest slums in Asia, as the area for training by actually building a powerful organization there.

Tondo was a squatter community on the Bay of Manila of several hundred thousand people, who had been displaced by the war and economic disruptions, including massive migrations of rural people seeking work in the cities. Many of the homes were built on stilts, necessitated by the rise and fall of the tides. Even though the government had passed legislation in the 1950s clearing the way for the land to be sold to those currently living on it, those title transfers never took place. In 1970 the Philippine government proposed a plan to expand the harbor by selling the land to developers and moving out the people living there.

ACPO trainers contacted leaders in the community who were vigorously opposed to the displacement. An organization came into being, named Zone One Tondo Organization (ZOTO). They were effective in mobilizing marches and actions to thwart efforts to confiscate land.

Through their vigorous efforts, they met leaders of the World Bank and government funders and delayed funds slated for harbor expansion until the Tondo residents were included in the planning process.

When a devastating typhoon hit Manila Bay in 1970, ZOTO was more effective than the government was in getting aid to the community. When Pope Paul visited the Philippines, ZOTO leaders met with him and challenged a local cardinal not to back business interests, but rather support the needs of those in his parishes facing eviction. ZOTO leaders met with President Marcos and succeeded in securing commitments for infrastructure and rehabilitation that would improve their community and ameliorate the situation of those who were to be displaced.

During their campaign, the government imposed martial law, fearful of groups they deemed "subversive." Leaders of ZOTO were arrested and harassed. ZOTO, by indigenizing the tactics of Alinsky style community organizing to its context, became a model for others in the country seeking community empowerment and self-determination.

In Mumbai, India, a squatter community named Daharavi with a population of 200,000 is adjacent to the city's central business district. Public officials and business leaders were interested in developing the increasingly valuable real estate of the area. Community leaders understood they needed power to prevent their community from being usurped by others' interests. The Christian Institute for Social and Religious Studies (CISRS) brought trainers from ACPO, the organizing training center in Manila led by Herb White, to help them build a community organization named PROUD. Over a three-year period several dozen leaders, many of them students and young people, drawn from the churches and other faith traditions, went through the training.

PROUD started to build the power to resist the urban renewal effort to expand the business district and displace the squatter community. When community latrines began to be demolished, the organization mobilized a "shit-in" with hundreds of residents blocking traffic and "doing their business" in the thoroughfare that divided Daharavi from the commercial district. The latrines were quickly replaced.

Eventually, the city recognized the organization and made seats for their leaders on the "community renewal planning committee." In addition, the World Bank, a partner with the business community in planning the Daharavi development, invited residents to their planning table. The inclusion of PROUD leadership succeeded in getting commitments to high-rise housing for Daharavi residents in the development plan and provisions for assistance in relocation. Small shop keepers were included in the business plan and these merchants were able to get loans and grants to relocate and re-build their businesses in Daharavi. Though the community organizing could not completely block the redevelopment, the community was able to play a significant role in mitigating the negative impact.

Partly as a result of successful organizing efforts in Daharavi and other UIM church initiatives in Nairobi, Manila, El Salvador, Seoul, and Rio de Janeiro, the World Bank was forced to examine its development policies affecting poor communities. They subsequently adopted a policy of including the people being affected by the development in the project planning and implementation. At the Second World Congress of the United Nation's Department on Human Habitation, which was created in response to feedback from community organizations, Jessica Fernandez, an ACPO organizer from Tondo, was the speaker at a plenary session on citizen participation. These initiatives in community organizing in various localities led the WWC UIM to give highest priority to encouraging congregation-based community empowerment efforts.

UIM invited experts in community organizing to visit, support, and evaluate the work of efforts in the region. Saul Alinsky visited five countries and afterwards met for a three day consultation with organizers from Asian organizations. He was challenged to think about organizing in more autocratic political settings versus the democratic contexts of North America. Monsignor Jack Egan of Chicago, a leading advocate for American Catholic church's involvement with organizing, traveled to Japan, Philippines, Korea, Hong Kong, and India where he spent time with Roman Catholic bishops in those countries to encourage their support of community organizing. He ended up his tour in Rome with an audience with the Pope, reporting on the organizing efforts across Asia. Veteran Chicago organizer Tom Gaudette also conducted an evaluation survey of the Asian community organizing projects.

The UIM regional offices in Tokyo, Nairobi, Mexico City, and Amsterdam were pivotal in identifying and supporting these empowerment efforts. These in-region staff fostered the relationships with the UIM funded community organizations and brought them together for learning and strategizing. Many of the 200 people who completed the APCO training program in Manila are now engaged in organizing in low-income communities in fourteen Asian countries.

## 5) Work to support the involvement of the churches in programs addressing international exploitation, especially by multi-national organizations.

One of the UIM grants supported an industrial mission project in Kenya. The project built on a legacy of industrial mission work that traced its roots back to British Anglican and Methodist missionaries. The most influential figure in the field was Ted Wickham, who was the bishop of a largely industrial diocese in England. In his book *Church and People in an Industrial City*, he envisioned a parish that was not geographical but vocational in its constituency. He assigned clergy as new church development pastors in steel mills. Taking their lead from his ideas, staff from the Kenya National Christian Council organized discussion groups and Bible studies with engineers, accountants, and clerks who worked in industrial and commercial enterprises.

Out of these discussions, they produced a book, *Who Controls Industry in Kenya?* which was edited by Sam Kobia. When it was first published, the book was banned by the government. It was accurately perceived as an expose and critical analysis of the continuing economic dominance that British corporations enjoyed in the post-colonial period. UIM often supported these types of investigative research efforts by ecumenical organizations in order to assist churches to understand better the economic and political dynamics in their country.

UIM was involved in the founding and original funding of the Interfaith Center for Corporate Responsibility, with some 75 interfaith organizations as members. ICCR monitors corporations relocating American plants to developing countries, labor practices in overseas plants, and the impact of such relocation on American workers. When the unjust working conditions of women in Korean textile factories was exposed, ICCR encouraged American denominations to use their power as stockholders to influence corporations doing business with those textile factories.

The European Council of Churches maintains an office in Brussels for monitoring the European Economic Union. Representatives of sponsoring churches meet frequently to review policies and practices of European industry in developing countries, as well as the ways immigrant workers are treated in Europe.

## 6) Facilitate sharing of experiences by Christians in socialist countries of UIM activities appropriate to their own context, as well as work similar in contexts around the world.

More than 340 Protestant, Anglican, Orthodox, and other communions are members of the World Council of Churches. A number of the member churches have congregations in countries with socialist governments. Some are in countries with autocratic regimes, which impose regulations and restrictions on churches, and often keep church activities under surveillance. Some socialist countries have more open societies and are less restrictive of church activities. In some countries, there are Marxist or anti-Marxist insurgencies pressing churches to make ideological choices. Many churches in socialist countries are eager to be in communication and fellowship with other churches in socialist societies and with churches in more democratic countries.

The WCC provided opportunities for participation from member churches in socialist countries to travel and be in communication with churches from other countries, if their governments allowed their participation. Most of the participants in UIM events came from Latin American, Asian, and African countries, but not Eastern Europe. Upon initiative from a number of eastern European countries, the WCC UIM was invited to participate in annual gatherings of churches from the Soviet sphere hosted annually in East Germany. Christians from Hungary, Poland, Romania, Czechoslovakia, Estonia, Lithuania, and the U.S.S.R gathered to share how their churches were involved in mission activity in large cities and with workers in industrial areas.

Sometimes these delegations were accompanied and monitored by government observers. These occasions provided unique opportunities for UIM church workers to meet each other across national boundaries. Sometimes participants shared how the government was helpful in providing jobs, education, and welfare for their people. Most churches were actively providing programs for youth, for those with addictions, for unwed mothers, and providing opportunities for people in neighborhoods to gather and discuss problems and issues. WCC reproduced the papers and reports of these annual gatherings in English, French, and Spanish for a worldwide audience.

Most regular gatherings of the UIM contact groups included participants from Asian, African, and Latin American socialist countries. Their representatives often triggered lively debates of the merits and deficiencies of socialist and capitalist societies. They pressed WCC UIM to include as a priority the concern for churches in socialist countries and valued their connection with church leaders in other countries. The whole work of the WCC benefited from their perspective and challenge.

The Sri Lanka Christian Worker's Fellowship has one of the longest histories of UIM participation and has given inspiration to other churches about how to work and worship in a socialist society. One example is the annual Worker's Mass. This May Day thanksgiving celebration was a joint service for all the Protestant denominations in the country's largest city, Colombo. Workers, both Christian and non-Christian, carry their tools, trade-marks, and other symbols of their work as an offering. Secretaries brought their steno pads, factory workers brought tools or machinery, and merchants their wares. They were joined by church members and paraded to the town hall and then to the church. The Eucharist began with the offering of bread and wine, as the crowds also offered the symbols of their work at the communion table. One "tool" brought to the table was a red flag, symbolic of Marxist thought and analysis. Living in a socialist nation they sought to see God's hand at work in the economy in which they labored. The offering was followed by confession, where the people acknowledged the ways that they have misused their gifts, admitting their personal shortcomings, as well as the failures of their society. The bread and wine were shared as gifts of God's forgiveness and redemption, making whole what is broken and incomplete. The service culminated with a charge to depart from the table and return to their lives and vocations with a commitment to work towards justice and human fulfillment. The workers received back the red flag and their work implements as they departed. Such experiments in new forms of worship have had an influence on the organized churches in Sri Lanka and elsewhere.

## 7) Encourage Biblical and theological reflection and articulation, giving priority to listening to the people, giving tongue to the language of the people, and sharing stories of the people.

For WCC UIM, theological and biblical reflection and articulation were not just the work of academic gatherings, but emerged from people's experience. Though theologians might give useful language to think about God in their own context, the theological reflection mostly came from people's *praxis* (lived experience) of faith in their own communities. Articulate voices from the developing world and their emerging theological frameworks called into question predominantly Eurocentric theology that had often been the consensus view in the WCC of the post World War II era.

The World Council of Churches was formed in 1948 at the zenith of Barthian theology, with its emphasis on the sovereignty of God and centrality of the Word. Among those engaged with ecumenical UIM activity, influences came from the Niebuhrs, Tillich, Bonhoeffer, Berdaev, Ellul, and Gollwitzer. By the 1960s, the whole of Western European theological thought was being challenged by emerging voices from around the world.

In an office like UIM, working in differing contexts throughout the world, it was evident there could be no single theological framework. Doing theology was necessarily contextual. New forms of ministry and theology emerged, shaped by the history and circumstances of those societies.

In Africa, urban and industrial ministries were seeking to preserve the values of tribal communalism in the mutual respect and caring rural peoples were bringing to their new urban situation. Theological reflection in African Christian communities embraced the reverence for ancestors and connections with the earth, which some missionaries often had required converts to reject. A new generation of African Christian theologians, educated in the West, but finding voice for their heritage, began to publish extensively and bring their analysis to the challenges facing their countries emerging from the colonial period.

Liberation theology, which articulates "the preferential option for the poor," emerged from the work of Latin American priests organizing Bible study groups in poor and working class urban and rural communities where they began to explore their experience through the liberation stories of the scriptures. In the Old Testament, the Exodus experience places God on the side of a people oppressed by an imperial power. The prophets hammer away at those in power when the poor are neglected and abused. In the New Testament, Jesus aligns the reign of God with the marginalized of his day. As they engaged with the Bible, the people began to articulate the tenets of liberation theology, which found a full theological treatment in *A Theology of Liberation* by Father Gustavo Gutierrez. Many activist parishes, across Latin America, often called "base communities," became advocates for worker's justice, equitable land distribution, addressing the incomes gap between the rich and the poor, and challenging the colonial lega-cies that shaped power arrangements. Liberation theology became an important emerging theology in seminary study, not only in Latin America, but around the world.

In Asia there also emerged in the 1960s and 1970s a number of new theological perspectives. Activities of the churches in squatter communi-ties, slums, and factory worker compounds in South Korea led to what is known as *Minjung Theology. Minjung* means "the people," especially those at the bottom of the society, the workers and the poor, but also the victims of injustice and those suffering oppression or deprivation. The term evokes a long-term historical and cultural feeling of shame in being poor and insists on the values and the rights of every human being.

Before the coming of Christ, the rich and the powerful were at the center of a society and the *Minjung* were on the periphery; then in the New Testament, the *Minjung* are at the center. Through Christ, God entered the life of the world by becoming incarnated in the *Minjung*. The body of Christ resides in on-going history through the struggle of the *Minjung* for liberation. Their story is the story of God's presence in contemporary history in its move toward liberation and fulfillment in the coming kingdom of God. A significant anthology of the leading Asian thinkers in this field was edited by Kim Yong-Bock and published by the Christian Conference of Asia (CCA). Kim described the work of UIM as an "international justice koinonia."

In India, in the 1970s and 1980s there emerges a unique *Dalit Theology. Dalit* was a word given to the untouchable caste, which represented about 20% of the Indian population, over 200,000,000 people. A large percentage of Indians who joined Christian churches were *Dalits* attracted to Christ's message that all people are God's children deserving honor and respect. Unfortunately, even the caste system thinking was evident in the Christian communities, where the *Dalits* sometimes were not afforded equal standing. As they read the scriptures, the *Dalit* communities discovered that God was with them in their struggle against prejudice, marginalization, and oppression. They believe that Jesus was a *Dalit*, born as an outsider, and his ministry can be seen through that lens. The cross has special meaning. There Jesus is broken, split open, rent asunder and reveals his *Dalitness*. Christians are called to identify with those marginalized, as the crucified Christ does with the *Dalit*.

In North America, both Black theology and Feminist theology were challenging neo-orthodoxy. James Cone, an African Methodist Episcopal pastor and scholar, created a stir with the publication in 1969 of *Theology and Black Power.* The hermeneutic, or interpretive lens, for Cone's theology starts with the experience of African Americans as slaves and the on-going racism of the dominant American culture and the church's complicity in that oppression. Mary Daly broke new ground for a feminist theology with the 1968 book, *The Church and the Second Sex.* The starting point of feminist theology is women's experience, and the rejection of 'patriarchy,' a male-dominated power structure throughout Western society and in individual relationships. Other challenging feminist theological voices were Rosemary Radford Ruether and Letty Russell.

Though there are common themes in many of these theological perspectives, it would be an injustice to the contextuality of each to attempt to blend them into one theology. Our intent was to encourage people in their context to deepen their own critical thinking and find occasion to share that with others.

In the post-colonial period in which the World Council was established, something profoundly new is occurring in world Christianity. Dozens of newly autonomous Christian churches in Asia, Africa and Latin America are sitting as peers with people from the historic European and North American churches. There was an inevitable "upsetting the applecart" for those whose Christian identity was bound by their historic European and North American denominations and creeds. But like Pentecost, there was an outpouring of new voices, dreaming dreams long held by their peoples. Though UIM was not a main locus of theological discussions in the WCC, it sometimes felt like the pub where Luther's reformation found its voice in the hubbub of people's experience.

## 8) Support persons suffering loss of human rights through repression because of their involvement in UIM.

Much of the UIM work was inherently political in character. Community organizing and labor movement solidarity often led to controversy, as the interests of the people challenged the existing order. In countries with military dictatorships and martial law, it was not unusual for UIM related activities to come under police and intelligence agency scrutiny. Offices were searched, people were followed, meetings infiltrated, leaders were imprisoned and abused, some were forced into exile, and others lost their lives. Twice regional group members were apprehended on their way to international UIM meetings. One leader was never found.

Park Hyung Kyu was chairperson for the Board of Yonsei University's Institute for Urban Ministry in Seoul, South Korea. He was the pastor of a nearby urban congregation. The Institute trained clergy and seminarians to work among poor people in industrial areas and squatter communities. Rev. Park was arrested and accused of treason against the repressive regime. At an open air Easter morning service, he prayed for the people of his country, for the dictator that repressed the people, for freedom, and for those who suffered under the current regime. Leaders of the service were arrested and interrogated. They pressured Park to confess that he had ties with North Korea and intended to overthrow the government. He was sentenced to three months. He was arrested a second time when student protests were staged and then sentenced to five years, followed by exile from the country. His church building was closed, but his congregation assembled every week in front of the boarded up church building to worship and pray. UIM groups around the world supported these efforts with prayers, financial support, and support for legal representation. Our office helped him in exile and provided support for study while in the U.S. Eventually he was able to return to Korea and his pastoral duties.

Canaan Banana was a Methodist minister in Zimbabwe who served a congregation and a community center in the city of Bulawayo. The country at the time was named Rhodesia and was ruled by the descendants of the British settlers that had colonized the country. He was selected by an

African regional group to be a representative at an Asian UIM conference and subsequently studied urban issues in twenty Asian countries. After returning to Africa, he immersed himself in the struggle for freedom of his country. He became a leader of one of the three primary resistance parties in Rhodesia and was imprisoned on several occasions.

UIM assisted him to study overseas and write a book *Prayers for the Struggle*, as well as helping his family. Upon his return from studying abroad, he was immediately imprisoned again. He was released to attend several meetings between the government and insurgent political parties, with international mediators, to broker peace and form a new government. When a settlement was achieved and independence came to what is now Zimbabwe, he was elected the first president. During the first year of independence, President Banana invited my son Sam, when he was at Yale Divinity School, to teach for a summer at the community center of his church where young people, who had dropped out of school to fight for independence, were catching up on their education.

Edicio de la Torre was a Catholic priest in the Philippines. He was associated with the community organizing training center in Manila, ACPO, especially with their work in Tondo. He was popular with young people as an artist, singer, and story-teller. He was deeply involved with political opposition to President Marcos. For these activities, he was imprisoned several times. In one incarceration, UIM was able to get the U.S. government involved on his behalf and he was offered release, if he would leave the country. After Marcos' defeat he returned to the Philippines, where he continued organizing and now directs an institute for democracy education for young people.

My travels, to support the WCC UIM work, were extensive, maybe a fifth of my time, and often for several weeks at a stretch. These responsibilities took me to Melbourne and Mexico City, to Berlin and Tokyo, to Nairobi and Bangalore, to Vancouver and Paris, and many other great cities around the world. Often within an hour of landing at the airport, I was among UIM partners who were working for justice with the poorest city residents, migrants, squatters, and unemployed. I happened to land in Manila the day ZOTO met with President Marcos. Upon my arrival, I was transported to the presidential office where leaders were negotiating their demands.

I was also grateful for the immersion in local cultures where our UIM partners worked with the chance to see local drama and film, enjoy indigenous dances and music, or collect carvings, weavings, or paintings from talented artisans. Kathy set a $15 limit on my purchases and even so our home is full of treasures, each with a story. The experience of worshiping in congregations throughout the world, in many cultures and languages, deepened my understanding of the faith and expanded my sense of the Spirit working in many remarkable ways - a global Pentecost.

Though my specific responsibilities were in urban and industrial mission, being a part of the WCC staff entailed many other involvements. Working for the WCC for ten years was an amazing immersion in the worldwide ecumenical church. Because I chaired the North American regional staff group, I was also a participant in weekly meetings with the General Secretary, Phillip Potter. That Staff Executive Group was the clearing house for program concerns and possibilities for the WCC.

With my interest in liturgy and music, I enjoyed the opportunity to participate in the worship life of the WCC. I helped plan worship for some annual meetings of the WCC Central Committee and the every eight years' meeting of the General Assembly, as well as the every ten years' Conference on World Mission Evangelism (WME). This entailed recruiting worship leaders from six regions to contribute music, prayers, liturgy and other worship materials. These multicultural worship experiences were published for use of member churches. The theme for one CWME conference was "Thy Kingdom Come." Churches of many countries offered hymns and songs on the "kingdom" theme. Fr. Jacques Bertier, of the Taize community, composed the song *Jesus Remember Me, When You Come into Your Kingdom*, which, using the words of the thief on his cross, stressed Christ's humility, not triumph. That musical contribution has wide usage throughout the church today.

During our time in Geneva, Kathy was employed by the international and ecumenical Frontier Internship in Mission program which shared an office with the World Student Christian Federation. As staff person she helped to coordinate a program that provided internships for young people with experience in social justice efforts, such as women's rights, racism, peace, and economic justice, to work in another country where similar concerns were being addressed. She was able to travel to WSCF and WCC conferences in Nairobi, Melbourne, Berlin, Harare, and London. She was also involved with the international school where our sons received an excellent high school education and participated in the WCC's Ecumenical Women's Group that monthly studied feminist writings and themes. Their studies led them to change the name of the WCC's traditional "Ecumenical Wives Group" to "Ecumenical Women."

We both enjoyed the beautiful Swiss countryside and the rich history so close at hand. We traveled together as a family on vacations to nearby European destinations. Kathy found the international community there extraordinarily stimulating, in that people from so many different places and cultures could share the bond of being a world-wide ecumenical Christian family.

In our Christmas letter from 1975, we described the WCC UIM work to family and friends this way:

*At this time we are especially remembering colleagues in programs in a number of countries, who because they identify with people who suffer poverty due to unjust social, economic, and political structures, and who because of their work to bring about changes, are suffering imprisonment, loss of political rights, harassment of many kinds, and sometimes exile. They ask us to join with them to work for an end to all exploitation and for the fulfillment of justice among all peoples and nations, as prophesied by Isaiah and Mary's Magnificat and as announced in Christ's words in the synagogue at Nazareth (Isaiah 40, 65:17-25, Luke 1:47-44, Luke 4:16-19)*

*We are astonished, inspired, and shamed by the joyful readiness of these men and women to suffer for their convictions. This is costly work demanding lives and vocations, as well as money. The facts of contemporary structures of power and the weight of events seemed ranged against the foolishness of saints and prophets like some of these.*

*Christmas is God's foolishness, to empty himself of omnipotence, risking incarnation as a baby in a working class family. Our son Peter sent this quotation, inspired by an e. e. cummings poem, in his first letter from college:*

*"how should the contented fools of facts
envision the mystery of freedom?
yet among their loud exactitudes of imprecision
(seeming enough for slaves of time and space)
ours is the here and now of freedom.
Come."*

Those on the staff of the WCC were called to three-year terms. To assure that over time the staff would reflect the diversity of the global church, one could serve a maximum of three terms, or nine years. In 1983 I came to the end of my third term and Kathy and I decided that it was time to return to the States. We felt it would be good to settle down near New York, as two of our sons were living in the region, either in college or working.

We especially felt the need to be closer to Peter who had become ill in college, struggling through bouts of schizophrenia. With all the uncertainties, emergencies, and responsibilities surrounding his illness, we could no longer effectively help him from overseas. We needed to move back to the USA.

I did not have a job lined up, but as always, I was hopeful for the opportunity to serve a local congregation. I never imagined I would be away from parish ministry this long working in church bureaucracies. We received a lump sum from monies accumulated in the WCC retirement plan which helped us purchase a house in Montclair, New Jersey, close to where we had lived before moving to Geneva. It seemed a good place to live and work somewhere in the greater New York area.

As had been the case all through my ministry, I did not find jobs, they seemed to find me. Even before I was clear about leaving Geneva, a Chicago foundation, Wieboldt, approached me about being their executive director. A colleague, Stanley Hallett, was on the board of the foundation and put forward my name for consideration. I was not then seeking a new position, but he urged me to talk with the board about the work they were doing and new directions they might explore. I left that conversation assuming they would be hiring someone else in short order.

We moved to Montclair in May of 1983. Our son John was getting married in Boston in late June. We were getting ready to leave for the wedding when the phone rang. It was the Wieboldt Foundation and they were still in the interviewing process and wanted to know if I would consider the position now. I flew out the next week to interview and they offered the job. Although we had already purchased our home in New Jersey, this seemed like a great opportunity. Their mission was to fund efforts which bettered life in Chicago, with special priority on community organizing. There had only been three executives in Wieboldt's 62 years of existence and the possibility of a long tenure and not having to travel as much was attractive. After working in large bureaucracies, the idea of being at the helm of a smaller organization and helping guide its directions was appealing. I had grown up in the Chicago area, having been raised in Gary. Kathy was open to the move, as we felt we would be able to support Peter from there. We moved to the Windy City in the fall of 1983.

# CHAPTER 6

— ✂ —

# Funding Change: The Wieboldt
# Foundation in Chicago (1981-1986)

THE WIEBOLDT FOUNDATION was established in 1920 by the German immigrant founder of what became one of the biggest department store chains in Chicago. William Wieboldt was a leading citizen, entrepreneur, and philanthropist. He came as an immigrant decades earlier with very little in the way of possessions, but the ambition to start a dry goods store. By mid-century, there was hardly a suburban mall in Chicagoland that did not have a Wieboldt department store as an anchor tenant. As he neared retirement, he and his wife Anna decided they would leave the bulk of their wealth to create a foundation benefiting the welfare of the people of Chicago, a city they felt indebted to for all they had received.

When I went to the foundation, the previous executive, Bob Johnson, had just retired after a 20-year tenure. As he was leaving, he wrote a book urging the foundation world to target support for community organizations. He believed that community organizing, which empowered people in the low income areas to shape the decisions being made about their own communities and about the city, was the best way that the Wieboldt Foundation could be faithful to its mission of supporting "charities designed to put an end to the need for charity."

Chicago was the birthplace and the incubator for the community organizing movement. In the decades since the 1930s when Saul Alinsky organized the Back of the Yards community and started the Industrial Areas Foundation, a number of community organizations had started, such as The Woodlawn Organization (TWO), the Northwest Community

Organization (NWO), and others. There were other organizing institutions that had started in the city such as ACORN and MAHA (Metropolitan Area Housing Association).

Johnson believed the Wieboldt Foundation had the opportunity as a small progressive foundation to break ground for other members of the foundation community to understand and support organizing. He facilitated the Wieboldt Foundation board's analysis of community issues by bringing urban experts like Stanley Hallett onto the board of directors. For most of its history, the board had been comprised entirely of family members. By the time I came, the board had increased in size to fifteen members, with seven being non-family members and eight from the family. They met at least once a month to make grant decisions. The staff would bring information and recommendations about the projects, but the board members actively evaluated proposals and decided on award levels.

I had known Hallett for many years in my urban ministry work and he was one of my heroes. Stan was a Methodist minister who went to Boston University Theological Seminary and was a pupil of Walter Mulder, a leader in the field of Christian ethics. Mulder played an important role in the formation of the World Council of Churches. He was one of the central figures in the development of a theology of the *responsible society* that informed the early years of the Council. Stan concurrently received a degree in Urban Planning. He went to the faculty of the Methodist related Garrett-Evangelical Theological Seminary on the Northwestern University campus in Evanston, a suburb just north of Chicago. Stan was a brilliant observer of city life and an inspirational teacher.

One interesting project Stan and I collaborated on was working with the Rouse Corporation, famous for the development of waterfront malls in Boston, New York City, and Baltimore. James Rouse bought hundreds of acres of land in a mid-way point between Baltimore and Washington, with a view toward building a "new town," a planned city, to become Columbia, Maryland. It was to have a population of 90,000. Rouse's urban design think-tank included urban planners, architects and engineers, but to the mix he added also philosophers, criminologists, sociologists, and other disciplines. They set out to envision "the ideal city."

The group had been working for two years before Rouse thought of inviting professionals with a religious perspective to participate. Stan Hallett from Garrett Theological Seminary, Kim Jefferson of the Methodist Church national staff, John Wagner of the National Council of Churches, and I were invited to sit on the working group. At the first meeting we attended, they briefed us on their plans to date, showing us their maps to explain their design. Kim asked politely, "Where is the cemetery?" They all looked at each other realizing they had not considered a cemetery in the design for their ideal city.

In particular, they were interested in our ideas on the dilemma of how the "new town" should be churched. They did not think it appropriate for a town invented from scratch to be dotted with new church developments of differing denominations, ostensibly competing with one another. How might they create a community supporting mutual understanding among religious communities? It was decided to build a multi-purpose religious complex in the town center – a chapel/temple that served as a Catholic church, a Protestant church, and a Jewish synagogue. The different communities worshiped at different times, but shared the same space, with a revolving worship table, that had a crucifix on one side, a cross on another and the Torah on another.

We also pushed the design team to consider the economic diversity of a healthy city, where people of differing incomes were not spatially segregated. They took these ideas seriously in the design of the community. Rouse subsequently hired Stan as the official historian of the development. Later, Stan came back to Chicago and taught on the faculty of the Urban Studies Department of Northwestern University. Hallett's expertise was indispensable as the Wieboldt board pursued its mission.

Being a relatively small family foundation, Wieboldt's corpus during my tenure ranged from $12 million to $16 million. Under law, the foundation was required to spend a minimum of five percent of the value of the corpus annually, which generally the board used as a benchmark to guide their giving. This was during the years of the Clinton presidency, when the stock market was performing well and regularly yielding between 8% to 12% return a year, so the corpus grew significantly.

We had several hundred thousand dollars in grant assistance to disperse each year, which was small compared to other large city foundations. The advantage to being small was a certain amount of agility and freedom. Wieboldt was viewed favorably by the local foundation community for its progressive vision, innovative approaches, and strong commitment to community-based organizations. My interest was to build on their previous work by further sharpening their definition of community organization. This resulted in their grants very specifically supporting congregation-based community organizing work in greater Chicago.

This was my first professional stint in the foundation world. I had much to learn about the philanthropic community. Chicago had a model Council of Foundations with a very capable executive who facilitated communication and interaction among the foundations. Staff persons and board members of other foundations were generous in sharing their experience with a newcomer on the scene. Based on my grant-making experience at the World Council, my commitment was to scout out and support organizations that were working at empowering communities for social change. With Wieboldt, several other likeminded foundations – Knight, Woods, and McArthur – worked collaboratively to pursue this strategy.

My daily work consisted of visiting and relating to the community organizing activity in the city. This included conversations with the organizers and leaders about their activities, their effectiveness, and organizational and financial well-being. It was my intention that the foundation be viewed as ally in their work, as well as funder.

By the 1980s the community organizing movement had been in existence for over 40 years. After Alinsky's death in 1972, the IAF continued under the leadership of Ed Chambers and Dick Harmon, who developed more systematic training for organizers and leaders of organizations. A network of IAF organizations emerged around the country, with Ernesto Cortez spearheading a strong network in Texas and other cities across the Southwest. Nationwide, the IAF has over 60 affiliates and conducts several ten-day training sessions annually for organizers and leaders.

Other community organizing networks came into being. DART, PICO, and the Gamaliel Foundation, each developed its own organizations and training. Altogether, there are some 175 congregation-based community organizations in urban and rural communities across the country.

As executive of the Wieboldt Foundation, I attended the annual Conference of the National Association of Foundations. In conjunction with some of the other Chicago based foundations that funded community organizing, there emerged opportunities at the national level to discuss the work of community organizing. This led to annual meetings of foundations interested in funding organizing and ultimately to the formation of the Neighborhood Funders Group. A Washington office was established with more than 100 foundations participating.

As proud as I was of the foundation's commitment to community organizing, one of the most interesting and satisfying projects that Wieboldt undertook in my time there was in the political realm. Chicago has a long history of "boss" government, with the long tenures of the Daley father and son. When Harold Washington, an African American Democratic candidate ran for mayor, there was high hope he could become the city's first black mayor.

After a successful primary, the Washington campaign people knew he stood a good chance of getting elected. In all likelihood, their camp, which had little experience in actually governing, would be taking the reins of the city. They started asking hard, practical questions, "What are the different city departments and who staffs them? What kind of talent is needed to fill positions and which ones in place should be retained?"

To get some answers, they went to the Urban Studies Department at the University of Illinois. The department chair, Richard Simpson, approached Wieboldt with a proposal. Simpson would utilize the faculty and students of his department to produce a handbook that could guide any new administration. Knowing of his work in urban policy at the university, I recommended funding this project and the foundation board concurred.

That Urban Studies group produced a detailed study of the Chicago city government. The report defined the task of every department, identified current commissioners or directors, explored the budgets of each department, and what were the current problems, issues, and challenges. As staffing the departments was a critical task of a new administration, the report listed the current staff persons, what were the qualifications needed, and which posts were typically political patronage appointments. When Washington was successfully elected, the university's report served as a workbook in guiding the first several months of the administration. The Wieboldt Foundation took satisfaction in having helped make that report possible.

During my tenure in Geneva I had remained a member of New York City Presbytery, but thinking this would likely be my last job until retirement, I transferred my membership to Chicago Presbytery. Wieboldt seemed to be the place we would be staying. Kathy and I were both active in the Chicago Presbytery and served on church committees.

Kathy had a busy career now that our sons were out on their own. One of the long-standing ecumenical training programs, the Urban Training Center, was in a leadership transition. Don Benedict, executive of the Chicago City Mission Society, which later became the Community Renewal Society, hired Kathy as interim director, while awaiting a new director who would not be available to start for another 12 months. Kathy organized a new board and a series of training programs during the summer and fall of 1982 and continued to work with the Urban Training Center after the permanent executive director came on board. Some time later, ICUIS, the news service and archive for the worldwide urban industrial mission, was in transition and Kathy was brought in as interim director.

The time in Chicago working for Wieboldt represented an especially rich period in our life. Our kids were up and out. I enjoyed the life of a foundation executive, a profession famous for being wined and dined, and was more than fairly compensated. This financial stability was welcomed in a time while three of our boys were in college or graduate school. We were also paying substantial support for Peter who was living full-time in a psychiatric treatment center.

Kathy and I were fortunate to find a lake-front apartment, on South Lakeshore Drive on the shore of Lake Michigan. This home was as fulsome a facility for a ministry of hospitality as any place we ever lived. Having come from the World Council to Chicago, we were delighted by the stream of friends and visitors coming to town from all over the world - Korea, Hong Kong, India, Taiwan, Brazil, Kenya, Mexico, Cameroon, Switzerland, as well as from all over the United States. This sharing of our home became a significant part of our life in Chicago and has continued unabated since.

Our apartment building bordered on Hyde Park, the home of the University of Chicago and a consortium of seminaries, which included McCormick Seminary. We soon became involved with three different congregations. When we went out the door of our apartment house and crossed to the other side of Lakeshore Drive, we were in the predominately black community of Woodlawn. An African-American Presbyterian congregation about two blocks away was the closest church for us to get to on Sunday. The First Presbyterian Church in Chicago, also in Woodlawn, was another several blocks away. This congregation, with Charles Leber and Buck Blakely as its pastors, was famous for its work with the Blackstone Rangers and the pioneering work of The Woodlawn Organization. I had long contact with that church from my time on the Board of National Missions. Kathy joined that congregation and we were both active there. Archie Hargraves, who had been an original member of the East Harlem Group Ministry in New York, was then the pastor of a United Church of Christ congregation only about five or six blocks from where we lived. We renewed our friendship with him and his wife, a delight after so any years together in the Group Ministry of EHPP. Archie continued the creative liturgy he had pioneered in East Harlem in this congregation.

Our expectation that we were now settled for the rest of our lives in the Midwest was not the way our lives worked out. While spending the holidays in New York City in December of 1983, on New Year's Eve, our son Sam, who was in his senior year at Yale Divinity School went to a party in New York City with his brother Adam. He was not feeling well and told his brother he was going downstairs to take a walk and get some air. He never returned to the party. After searching for him most of the night, Adam called us. The police were contacted when it became clear he was missing. They began an investigation and we began to organize a search in the city with the help of hundreds of friends, college and seminary classmates, and concerned people who heard about his disappearance. Police later described it as one of the most comprehensive missing person searches ever undertaken in New York City. We remained in New York for most of that month of January coordinating the search. The Wieboldt Foundation leadership was generous in giving us all the time we needed during this crisis. The office had a capable assistant who kept operations going and board members covered some of the work load.

The leadership of the New York City Presbytery became aware of our circumstances and offered a large meeting room in their office at First Presbyterian Church as a headquarters for the search effort. Many people from local churches joined the effort and kindly supported us. Weeks passed, still with no sign of Sam, and we had to accept that he was gone, although we hoped against hope that he was still alive and would somehow turn up. There was never any evidence of foul play, so there is the possibility that he is still alive, but somehow cut off from us.

After a month, Kathy and I returned to Chicago, but continued to be involved in the efforts to locate Sam. My work with Wieboldt continued for another couple of years, but the need to be closer to the other boys weighed on both of us and the pull to be back in New York intensified. Another consideration in thinking about my vocation was some unease I was experiencing in laboring in a job outside the church. Though the foundation was a great place to work, and Wieboldt's mission was aligned with my vocational commitments, not working in the context of the church after 30 years felt somewhat strange.

At that time the presbytery executive of New York City Presbytery retired and the presbytery was in the midst of a search for new leadership. Several colleagues urged me to place my name in consideration. My good friend Bob Davidson, pastor of New York's West Park Presbyterian Church, impressed upon me that after all my urban ministry experience, nothing would be a more fitting final chapter to my career than serving the Presbyterian Church in the largest metropolitan center in the country. Our boys thought it was a good idea, as they were all living in the East, and Kathy concurred. To move things along, my son Adam came to Chicago with the necessary paperwork to sit me down and fill out the required forms. When he hand delivered the application to the search committee of New York Presbytery, it became real to me this might be my next calling.

I had conversations with the board members at Wieboldt about these possible changes before applying for the presbytery position. They were very sympathetic to whatever I thought best for my family and gracefully indicated they would not feel cheated if I accepted the position.

In my interview with the Presbytery search committee, the discussion was constructive and the possibilities of working as the executive presbyter in this most urban of contexts were energizing. The position was offered and I gratefully accepted. We sold our apartment and made the move in the winter of 1986. Kathy and I found ourselves returning to New York City which had been home for much of our life together.

## CHAPTER 7

—— ❧ ——

# **Urban Ministry Writ Large:** Return to New York City Presbytery (1986-1992)

My work as Executive Presbyter of New York City Presbytery began in January of 1986. My previous efforts in congregations, community organization, industrial and urban mission, denominational and international agencies and the foundation world provided a well of experience to draw upon in serving on the presbytery staff of the nation's largest city. The presbytery's bounds are the five boroughs, so by definition every one of the one hundred and ten congregations was urban. I welcomed being back in the midst of this vibrant urban setting and working among our Presbyterian churches as they witnessed to the kingdom of God in their life and work.

Being a member of New York City Presbytery since 1953, except for our brief stay in Chicago, the lay of the land was familiar and I had known many of the clergy and congregations and members for many years. As I sat down at my desk that first day, I felt excited and challenged to be working with this presbytery in facing a set of critical questions. How could the presbytery wisely discern God's intentions as to what its appropriate mission might be? As the presbytery addressed the challenges of its communities and city, how could it provide adequate resources? In the midst of change and transition, how can congregations sustain health and vitality? How can the newly restructured presbytery represent its diversity of congregations, communities, and ethnicities? Finally, how can the presbytery explore new and imaginative shapes of ministry?

In regard to the question of institutional forms, ever since my days in East Harlem I had been open to what new forms the ministry of the church might explore in addition to that of the traditional local congregation. When I was with the Board of National Missions in the Presbyterian Church in the 1960s, the World Council undertook a study entitled *The Missionary Structure of the Congregation*. That study questioned whether in a fast changing world the primary shape of Christian community could continue to be the local geographical parish. The local congregation's organization, building, resourcing, and sustainability consume a great deal of a congregation's energy. In the study, they adopted the term "morphological fundamentalism" to describe how since the Reformation the congregation was almost the exclusive form of Christian community and could become more inward focused than mission driven. What new shapes might the church take? Some of those new shapes were explored in the industrial mission efforts where people gathered out of a shared vocation or interest. A whole range of experimental forms like apartment house ministries, shopping center ministries, industrial mission, and intentional communities like EHPP and the Iona Community had sparked people's mission imagination.

Having expressed my openness to new forms of Christian community, let me also affirm my deep belief that congregations remain basic to the shape of the church in the city and a relevant expression of God's intentions for humanity. During all my years of growing up and in my ministry with congregations, first experienced in Greenwich Village and East Harlem and then in a variety of urban settings all around the world, I knew personally how essential weekly worship and life together are, as we are shaped by God's word and formed by Christian community. At communion, we approach a table where all that we need as humans is provided by a loving God. As we break bread and share a cup with each other, we celebrate the Christ with us, the Christ in us, and the creation Christ infuses with meaning. At that table we offer ourselves, both our strengths and brokenness, knowing we need absolution, forgiveness, lifting of burdens, and the new possibilities Christ offers for each of us to be instruments for living out the will of God in the life of the city.

These activities might be seen as just the routine day-to-day life in an urban church, but they constitute the very essence of urban ministry. Urban ministry is sometimes too narrowly defined as programs for homeless and hungry people, powerful community organizations, or preschool programs. When ordinary local congregations incarnate the spirit of Christ in such a way that others remark, "See how these Christians love one another and the stranger," that is authentic urban ministry. The intention of a presbytery is to nurture urban ministry like this, in congregational life and in other expressions.

The best commentary of my attempts to support such urban ministry comes in the highlights of a report I made on the "State of the Mission" a few years into my tenure as Executive Presbyter:

"Fathers and Mothers, Sisters and Brothers, it is the responsibility and privilege of the Executive Presbyter to bring an annual *State of the Mission* report at the Annual Meeting. With other members of the staff, it is my regular responsibility to meet with the more than 30 Committees and Working Groups in this presbytery and to move among the 110 congregations, joining with members of churches as we celebrate anniversaries, honor pastors and leaders, call and install new pastors, carry on special events in works of evangelism, mission, music, or education. It is from that special vantage point that I speak to you today.

"After three years with this presbytery as its executive, I still feel somewhat uneasy with this title, Executive Presbyter. The name puzzles many of our older members and is even more mystifying to people from other denominations. Most community people say, "Oh, you mean it's like a Bishop?" Then I find myself explaining that the Presbyterian Church does not have a single person invested with a Bishop's authority, but that we do in fact have Bishops – the presbytery itself in our case, this body of 110 congregations is, in Presbyterian polity, our collective Bishop. Each congregation is under the authority of that Bishop. Every congregation participating as part of the collective so-called

'Bishop' carries the responsibility for the welfare and faithfulness of all the other congregations of our presbytery.

"The Executive Presbyter's job is to assist the presbytery to function and act like the Bishop, that it is, in appointing and installing clergy, caring for the welfare of every congregation, and helping the presbytery and its congregations to exercise prophetic gifts to say "no" to injustice and corruption and to hold out a vision of God's will for the possibilities of this city.

"Today, I want to offer a kind of audit as a way to review how we are doing in performing our tasks as a Presbytery. I wish the picture I'm presenting could be simpler, and more immediately comprehensible than it is. Yet, as I prepared this communication, I was again, myself, amazed at the diversity and interesting character of our life as a presbytery. Therefore, what I must offer is a kind of Byzantine mosaic which I hope may provide an overall design that will have some meaning and some beauty.

"Our congregations: Who are we? One hundred and ten congregations. 21 in the Bronx; 27 in Brooklyn; 27 in Manhattan; 31 in Queens and 4 on Staten Island. Twenty-nine of these congregations are predominately African-American; 17 Hispanic; 10 Korean; 2 Chinese; 1 is French-speaking, with its members coming from West Africa and Haiti; 21 of the predominately Anglo congregations have more than 25% of their members coming from other ethnic groups. Thirty-five congregations have a membership of less than a hundred people; 35 are 100 to 200 members; 31 are 200 to 500 members; and 2 are between 500 and 1,000. There are 3 congregations with between 1,000 and 2,000 members and 1 with over 2,700 members.

"We have 256 Minister Members. 98 of our 256 clergy members are giving a major part of their time as pastors of local congregations. Among the others – 49 of our pastors are retired; 22 are teachers or administrators in universities, schools, or seminaries; 11 are chaplains to hospitals, prisons, or military; 8 are full-time professional counselors. Thirty-six work with state, national or international agencies; 5 are Fraternal Workers of the denomination working in other countries. 32 more are in a wide variety of assignments ranging from writing and editorial work to investment counseling. Forty-one congregations currently do not have installed pastors.

Membership. Unfortunately, our presbytery's membership rolls have declined steadily in recent decades, though the rate of decline has decreased. Currently, our membership is slightly over 23,000.

Mission. Finally, we need to ask where has the presbytery been in relation to critical issues about suffering, injustice, and human need in New York City? I have used most of my time today talking about institutional and bureaucratic housekeeping matters. I hope these things have to do with the health of our congregations and the health of the presbytery. However, if they only serve to shore up our own internal fellowship of worship and spiritual rapport and have nothing to do with how we respond to the demands of God for realizing justice and peace on earth, then we are dry bones and not apostles of faithful service. Where has our presbytery been in relation to issues of hunger, housing, homelessness, public education, employment, disarmament, Central America, Africa, and responsible government? Today we honor Martin Luther King, Jr. We need to remember that his concern for justice for all people made him, in the words of J. Edgar Hoover, 'the most dangerous leader in the land.'

Here are some highlights of the ways our presbytery has actively engaged in its mission to the city:

- Through the initiative of our South Africa Task Force the Presbytery hosted Rev. Alan Boesak of Capetown and president of the World Alliance of Reformed Churches. 1,000 Presbyterians gathered to hear his biblical call to end apartheid

- Five busloads from the presbytery participated in the April demonstrations in Washington against U.S. policies in Nicaragua and South Africa.
- Ten congregations serve as feeding stations and food distribution centers.
- Seven congregations are involved with New York City Housing Partnership, which houses 1500 people a night in space provided by more than 200 congregations.
- The presbytery is a founder and sponsor of the Interfaith Assembly on Housing and Homelessness.
- Fifteen congregations are actively involved, along with other congregations, in renewing their communities through vital community organizations, each made up of coalitions of twenty to fifty congregations.
- The presbytery continued its long-standing commitment to criminal justice through its support of the Citizens Action for Justice Program and through the Church of Gethsemane. Two years ago the presbytery sponsored the development of a new congregation with the focus of enlisting members from the community of women who had been in prison.
- The presbytery continues to be in solidarity with gay and lesbian people. A large delegation participated in the Gay and Lesbian March on Washington last year.
- Every Wednesday night, More Light services are well attended. One congregation houses a feeding program for house-bound AIDS patients, which has subsequently become the largest program doing that in New York City.
- There is also an Aging Ministries unit with 34 congregations which serve as centers for friendship and caring for older people. A task force of the presbytery has been working on additional recommendations for enhancing our aging ministries."

I ended that report by saying, "I have attempted to paint a picture for you of a dynamic presbytery, productively struggling with an incredible variety of internal and external issues. I have tried to celebrate with you some of the ways that you – the Bishop – our presbytery, are caring for the church and for God's people. Through enabling ministries – through providing ways for us to care for one another – you are a corporate Bishop. Give your blessing to this presbytery and its congregations. May you all be numbered among the saints."

I found that the Executive Presbyter's job is often dominated by two rather prosaic tasks - being a real-estate manager and a personnel director. First, the majority of the buildings of our congregations are fifty to one hundred years old and often in need of serious maintenance. That meant working with congregations to keep a roof over their heads, repair or replace ancient boilers, keep the facilities up to city building codes, and find the resources, both technical and fiscal, to accomplish that. The job also involved the negotiations of the sale of some of these properties, and not only the church buildings, but also manses, community centers, and other properties.

The other big demand is functioning as a personnel officer. Here the Executive Presbyter works in close cooperation with the Committee on Ministry. Much of this work was helping congregations find full-time installed clergy or interim pastors or pulpit supplies. The job requires being a talent scout in searching for capable clergy for congregations and making opportunities for clergy in our midst to enhance their skills. There is a great deal of work that surrounds a pastor leaving or retiring from a congregation and the church preparing for new leadership.

There are also inevitable situations where there is conflict in a church, sometimes between factions in a congregation and other times when some people become disgruntled with a pastor. Some of these difficulties can be remedied quickly with a competent intervention, but some drag on indefinitely, leaving scars that may take years to heal. Besides the needs of the institutions for personnel assistance, there are also the

256 clergy members and their personal and professional concerns. Being a pastor to pastors is a large calling in itself. In addition, there was a talented Presbytery staff to nurture as a collaborative team and to create with them a healthy work climate.

Another big piece of the job of a Presbytery Executive, along with property and personnel, is finance. Budgets are the practical way we live out our commitments. To build a budget for the presbytery, one needs to find out what kinds of resources are available, what are the sources of support from the congregations, what monies might be accessed from the national church, as well as other ways to generate money to support the congregations and their ministries. In a presbytery of this size, it was no small job to engage the constituency of the presbytery in creating, approving, embracing, and supporting such a budget.

When I came, some of the presbytery's financial mechanisms needed attention. Many of the congregations were not paying their *mission apportionments*, a percentage of the church budget to help support the mission of the larger church, or their *per capita*, an assessment for each member on the church rolls to pay for administrative costs of the larger church. A portion of each of these two funds also provided support for the Presbytery. The presbytery also sponsored a group insurance policy covering many congregations' buildings. A number of churches had not been paying their fair share. A stewardship committee visited with every church to explore their own financial needs and possibilities, as well as their support of the Presbytery and larger church. The committee worked with congregations on assuring they had adequate insurance and good fiscal policies in place for handling the congregation's resources.

On the spending side of the equation, the Presbytery disciplined itself not to approve of programs that did not include provisions for funding them. By bolstering the income and tightening the reins on expenditures, the Presbytery, which had been running a deficit of $150,000 to $200,000 each year for five years, balanced its budget and no longer had to tap into reserves.

All these activities were happening because of the unheralded work of the some 300 clergy and laity that filled out the ranks of the 30 presbytery committees charged with the support of congregations and service to the world. Part of the hard work of the presbytery staff is the mundane, but time-consuming chore of keeping the trains running on time. Staffing these committees and supporting their effectiveness was one of the primary responsibilities of my first few years on the job. Our church governance stipulates that all our committees be representative of the diversity of our constituency. That means every committee needed a mix of clergy and lay people from all five boroughs, with age and gender diversity and fairly representing all our ethnic constituencies. It was at times tedious work, but the Stated Clerk of the Presbytery, a Committee on Representation, and I worked diligently in the belief that a strong committee of diverse interests is fertile ground for the work of the Spirit.

Of course, the ministry of this presbytery is most tangibly carried out at the congregational level. In a city of the remarkable diversity of New York, it is no surprise that there is a wide range of congregations. There are a handful of large congregations over 1,000 members that serve as beacons to the whole city with strong preaching, inspiring worship, large staffs, extensive programs, and significant resources. They provide education, cultural opportunities, and service to the larger community. There are also many smaller congregations, 100 to 300 members, scattered throughout the five boroughs of the city who are faithful to their community with the resources God has given them, which are sometimes very humble.

One such parish, The Gethsemane Church, focused its ministry toward women exiting prison, who often feel uncomfortable in more traditional church settings. The leaders of the effort approached the presbytery about using a vacant church building to house this outreach to newly released, incarcerated women and their families. Other congregations lent members for the startup of this effort and many of them were so committed to the work that they stayed. Every Sunday in worship there are prayers for men and women who are in local prisons and those on death row across the country.

In the South Bronx, five congregations are part of a coalition of 35 congregations that belong to the South Bronx Congregations (SBC), a congregation-based community organizing effort affiliated with the IAF network. They have identified and addressed such community concerns as affordable housing, public education, police protection and at-risk youth. Members of each congregation have participated in local and national leadership training programs where they have gained skills in public leadership not only to SBC and its initiatives, but to their local congregations. This organization has rehabilitated tenements and built hundreds of single family homes, known as Nehemiah Homes, which stabilized their communities and provided affordable housing and home ownership opportunities. One congregation, St. Augustine, in partnership with the presbytery, built a pioneering residence for grandparents who are raising their grand-children. Altogether, some 15 congregations of the presbytery are involved in congregation-based community organizing.

First Presbyterian Church of Jamaica is the oldest congregation in the presbytery having been established in 1662. The neighborhood had gone through many changes over the centuries, but the church has always been an important part of the community fabric. Its original building also served as the town hall for the community. The first lending library in New York was initiated by the church. The first primary school for African-American children in NYC began here. Today, this church is arguably the most multi-ethnic church in the presbytery with 25 to 30 nationalities represented in worship on a Sunday morning. In recent years, the church has focused ministry on children and youth, assisting young people in succeeding in school and helping make a pathway to college.

Lafayette Avenue Church in Brooklyn has a long distinguished history of involvement in significant social movements, including being a part of the Underground Railroad during the Civil War, the suffragette movement for women's votes, and more recently global labor justice issues through its work in creating a national organization of congregations, called The People of Faith. They advocate and bring pressure to bear on corporations for fair labor practices. Recently, the church gymnasium has become a popular off-Broadway theater performing dramas with religious and social justice themes.

The congregations that make up this presbytery are to be commended for their relationships to each other and to the other hundreds of congregations of different traditions that make up the whole body of Christ in New York City. Many of our congregations generously share their experiences and resources with one another. Beyond the Presbyterian family, New York City has had an active Council of Churches for decades and congregations have lent leadership and financial support for that ecumenical work. The Council has been an effective instrument for churches to influence the cultural and political dynamics of the city.

At least once a month, the chief executives (bishops, executive presbyters, district superintendents, etc.) of the governing bodies of ten denominations gather in the office of the Episcopal Bishop. Here there would be an exploration of issues unfolding in the city - political, economic, and cultural - and collective strategizing for addressing those concerns. Out of these deliberations came initiatives like the Interfaith Coalition for Housing and Homelessness and efforts to advocate with public officials in times of labor disputes.

I believe that none of my previous jobs - East Harlem, Taiwan, Board of National Missions Urban Office, World Council of Churches Urban Office, and the Wieboldt Foundation – was as demanding as being the Presbytery Executive of New York City. The constraints of being a Presbytery Executive were severe. Sometimes people talk of "an impossible job" being one where you have the responsibility, but not the authority to see the mission through. A good friend, Phillip Young, who had worked with me on the Board of National Missions and went on to be a presbytery and synod executive scolded me for not consulting with him when considering the job. "I thought we were friends," he said, "and you turn up as New York City Presbytery Executive, but you never talked to me before you went. I could have told you what the limitations, as well as the stresses and strains of that job are, and I would have strongly advised you not to do that." In retrospect, it is probably good I missed that advice before going in!

When I was hired, I signed a five-year contract. It was coming up for review when I began to experience significant health issues. I continued working, while the doctors ran tests, until it was decided that open heart surgery was necessary on my mitral valve. The doctors informed me the surgery would incapacitate me for two to three months. I took health leave, as provided in our Personnel Manual, and named colleague Jim Speer to be the Acting Presbytery Executive. The doctors told me, after the surgery, "We would advise you, if you are able financially, to retire at this point." I was 65 at the time and eligible for pension and Social Security, but I had not intended to retire for three more years. The doctors said, "Your body is like a used car that has undergone various repairs and will never be fully operational. You'll have to live with the consciousness of your limitations." I was not ready to hear that advice.

At the end of about two and a half months, I went back to work, but started experiencing blackouts. I would faint while walking down the street and wake up in a minute or two with a huddle of people around me asking "Are you all right, sir?" and I would have a hole in each knee of my trousers. Even so, I kept on working, until one day I blacked out in a staff meeting and it became obvious to everyone, including me, that this could not continue. I remember saying to myself, "I think maybe Jesus is telling me something." I listened and decided to retire.

The Personnel Committee of the presbytery was extremely supportive throughout my heart troubles and surgery. When it became clear that I should retire they were more than generous in the departing compensation package.

The New York City Presbytery voted on my retirement in September of 1991. At the Presbytery meeting where my retirement was accepted, there were kind speeches remembering the places that we had served along the way and the rich relationships that we enjoyed. The presbytery voted to extend the honor of naming me "Executive Presbyter Emeritus" and paid me generously through the end of 1992. As Kathy and I were retiring after almost 50 years of service to the church, we were both humbled by the privileges afforded us and the many places we served. It was fitting that the retirement was celebrated in New York City, as no place had called from me or given to me as much as this city had over the decades.

At the age of 67, I was now officially retired. Not finished, just retired.

# CHAPTER 8

— ✧ —

# A View From 21G: Busily Retired (1992 - Present)

LEAVING THE PRESBYTERY job when I did was necessary for my health. It was also a good step into the next part of my life. It took a full year until the doctors were able to stabilize my condition so that I stopped blacking out. By that time I began to realize that being retired was not such a bad thing. I was ready to appreciate the freedom which retirement offered to be with my family and to enjoy, more fully than I ever had before, quality time with friends, reading as much as I wished, and savoring the art, music, theater, and lectures the city affords.

Recently someone asked me about the small collection of Dodo birds that nest on one of my bookshelves. It struck me that this extinct bird and my collection of snails, are the animal gifts that seem to define my retirement. I think of the snail as methodical and measured, not really slow. With my heart condition I simply cannot run at full speed all day. If the day has three blocs of time – morning, afternoon, evening – I must rest at least one bloc, and sometimes two, out of a day. I try to pace myself to be able to do the things I enjoy without too much wear and tear.

As for the Dodo bird, I am grateful not to be extinct just yet. My mortality is not something I fear, as my life is in God's good hands. My generation, excessively credited by Tom Brokow as "The Greatest Generation," is certainly edging toward extinction however. Reading obituaries is always sobering and some of my excursions out these days are to say last good-byes.

As our dwelling place has always been important for us, one of the joys for Kathy and me is the wonderful high-rise apartment we inhabit in Morningside Gardens in Manhattan's Upper West Side. From the balcony of the 21st floor, we look south, over the tower of St. John the Divine Cathedral, all the way to the end of Manhattan with a glimpse of the spires of the Chrysler Building and the Empire State Building. Missing from that view now are the tops of the World Trade Center Towers. On that lovely September morning in 2001, I saw a low-flying jet hit one of the towers from our apartment balcony followed by billowing columns of smoke, rising flames, and then the collapse of the two buildings. Watching this apocalyptic scene unfold, I took down some volumes of illuminated manuscripts from our bookshelves depicting "the fall of the city" in the Book of Revelation, but the devastation was far more catastrophic than even the artist's imagination.

Looking west in our immediate neighborhood we see the Gothic tower of the Riverside Church. A bit farther south, we can view the Interchurch Center, the architectural "Godbox" where Kathy and I both worked for many years for the Presbytery of New York and the National Council of Churches. The Columbia University campus sprawls out below. The Hudson River courses by and the airspace above is busy with planes and helicopters. Kathy can see, only two blocks away, the Horace Mann Elementary School she attended for her first year of schooling and Union Seminary where she completed her last year of formal education. To the east we see the buildings of East Harlem, Mt. Sinai Hospital where three of our sons were born, and tantalizing glimpses of Central Park. The square footage in our apartment is limited, but its walls are lined with books, art from our travels around the world, and treasures from people and places we have known and loved. We are thankful for such a congenial space to call home.

Our Morningside Gardens housing project was a pioneer in establishing a NORC, a Naturally Occurring Retirement Community. Under state and city programs, if a housing complex can demonstrate that a certain percentage of its population is over 50 years old, it can receive subsidies to establish a senior center which provides services enabling people to "age in place." Seniors can continue to live in their homes and receive medical assistance, transportation to doctor's appointments, and access to social workers and a full-time nurse along with educational and recreational opportunities. Kathy has served on its Board and on several committees. We are part of a group of residents who call themselves "The Feet Firsters" because we anticipate not leaving until we are carried out.

One of the most rewarding aspects of our life continues to be a constant stream of visitors coming from all over the world. These are friends and colleagues we have known over the course of our lives and with whom we have worked, shared joys and sorrows, and served together in ministries of compassion and justice. I marvel at the faithfulness, creativity, and accomplishment of those who come by for coffee or lunch or to stay overnight. It is not uncommon in a month to enjoy visitors from Asia, Africa, Europe, Latin America, as well as from many parts of the United States.

In my retirement, I was to discover that in New York City there are four or five Shakespeare productions running on or off Broadway any given week. A diligent following of listings might make it possible to see Shakespeare's entire corpus of 38 plays in a year. I remember fondly that my father used to punctuate conversations with Shakespeare's quotes. When we were traveling and he was not so impressed by a destination, he might quote *As You Like It*, "So, this is the forest of Arden. When I was at home, I was in a better place." He'd quote the poem addressed to the heroine of the same play if we were behaving badly, "The sweetest nut hath sourest rind, such a nut is Rosalind."

In 1978, when I had to make three difficult journeys to New York from Geneva to tend to the crises surrounding the illness of our son Peter, I undertook to read the entire works of Shakespeare to allay some of my anxiety. My own attachment to the Bard was cemented through that challenging time.

In the late 1980s, one New York City company undertook to present sixteen versions of Hamlet, including the three original versions from

Shakespeare's hand, a 17th century German version, and the script of the TV show Gilligan's Island where the castaways attempt to present the play. For my perseverance in attending every production, the cast and director presented me with the skull that had been used for the graveyard scene. Often when friends visit, we see a production of Shakespeare in the Park or an off-Broadway interpretation. I am even sometimes persuaded, especially when Trey Hammond came to town to work on the book, to recite a soliloquy on the subway or bus on the way to or from the performance.

My retirement has not been entirely sybaritic. In the early 1990s, in conjunction with the Presbyterian Urban Ministry Office, I conducted a survey, directed by an overture to the General Assembly, of ways that Presbyterian congregations and presbyteries around the country were involved in affordable housing efforts and programs for people experiencing homelessness. My travels took me to more than 20 cities. It was interesting and a privilege to be able to discover how many Presbyterian individuals and congregations were actively engaged in addressing homelessness and affordable housing. Even a $600,000 portion of the Presbyterian Foundation portfolio was earmarked for investment in affordable housing. I helped organize a national conference bringing together housing advocates and activists who produced a draft of a pronouncement and policy statement on housing which was adopted by the General Assembly.

I have also been invited to attend national gatherings of Presbyterian clergy involved in congregation-based community organizing. There is increasing attention being paid to the community organizing movement by academic communities and a number of books have been written in recent years. One of these authors, Dr. Richard Woods of the University of New Mexico, was a keynote speaker at one of our meetings. These gatherings celebrated and encouraged the involvement of congregations in organizing, both in their internal ministries as well as in their relationships to their communities. The Presbyterian Church continues to be one of the largest Protestant funders of congregation-based community organizing through funds received in the One Great Hour of Sharing offering taken annually by local congregations. Several hundred Presbyterian congregations are member institutions of community organizations across the country and are addressing critical issues in their contexts.

Kathy has kept much busier in these retirement years than I, both in employment and volunteer efforts. When we moved back from Chicago, she was hired by the National Council of Churches and worked there for 14 years. Initially in 1988 she worked on an event observing the Millennial Celebration of the founding of the Russian Orthodox Church. Her job was to recruit and coordinate visits to the Soviet Union of ten large groups of American Christians to participate in this international ecumenical observance. As groups returned, they were debriefed and their reports were circulated to share their experience more widely. These visits were especially important before *glasnost* and *perestroika,* when it was not as easy for Americans to travel to the Soviet Union. The NCC had connections with religious communities in Russia allowing such visits that helped both countries, through citizen diplomacy, to move towards a post-Cold War understanding.

When this program ended, she organized and led travel and international exchanges to the Philippines, South Korea, and Cuba. She also worked for a couple of years with a National Council of Churches "New World Order" program, which worked at envisioning the changes possible with the end of the Cold War. After two years, this project was phased out and she went to work for the NCC's Europe Office where she served as Interim Director for nine months. When the NCC Europe Office was absorbed into Church World Service, Kathy continued with CWS until she retired in 1996.

In 1998, Kathy was asked to come back to the NCC as interim staff for the International Justice and Human Rights office, which was also merged into Church World Service. Over the next four years she worked on various projects including *Pillars of Peace for the 21ˢᵗ Century*, a statement developed through a number of regional consultations by the National Council of Churches in support of the United Nations. A second project she coordinated was an educational promotion, "Building a Culture of Peace with Justice," which publicized the work of four national and international church-related peace organizations. Kathy retired from the NCC in 2002.

As a volunteer, for several years she was the chair of the Global Justice and Peace Committee of Riverside Church and was also active in the environmental program of the church. She serves on the Board of the local senior center. She also serves as co-chair of the US Trustees of the World Student Christian Federation and is involved in fund-raising efforts for this 115-year-old international ecumenical organization that has been instrumental in shaping so many of us over the generations.. She also served for a number of years at the United Nations as a non-governmental organization (NGO) representative for the World Student Christian Federation and the National Council of Churches. She was also instrumental in starting a monthly discussion group at the Senior Center focusing on U.S. foreign policy and international issues related to the UN.

Once I had retired, we were invited by various friends we had worked with in Asia over the previous 20 years, to come and visit. We made two trips, one in 1996 and the other in 1998. The first trip was to Japan, South Korea, and Taiwan to join in special occasions with organizations where we had worked previously. One of those organizers was Masao Takenaka of the Evangelical Academy in Kyoto. He invited us to their 40th anniversary and asked me to make a presentation on *The Future of the World Church.* We were honored to have an art exhibition that was dedicated to us as a part of the festivities.

The second leg of that trip was to South Korea. During the Korean War, the Presbyterian Church was involved in founding a chain of orphanages in Korea and mobilized American churches to assist those orphaned by the conflict. In the 1960s, after the orphanages had accomplished their initial task, they were sold by the church. Under Korean law, they were not permitted to expatriate any of the proceeds. So, COEMAR found itself with a significant amount of money that had to be spent in Korea. Some of the proceeds were given to the Urban Office to subsidize the founding of the first Department of Urban Studies in Korea at Yonsei University in Seoul. The Head of the Public Administration Department, Dr. Ro Chung Hyun, was an active Presbyterian layman who had been subsidized by COEMAR's Leadership Development Program in getting his Ph.D. at New York University in Public Administration. He went back to Korea to serve on the faculty at Yonsei University. He was instrumental in establishing that Department of Urban Studies. One of the mandates of the department was to provide training to clergy and Christian leaders for work in urban ministry.

Herbert White was brought to the staff of that department to work on developing urban training for the church, especially using the model of community organizing. He had been head of staff for the Rochester Urban Ministry where he gave leadership in founding the IAF organization FIGHT. Kathy and I visited the Urban Studies Department and were able to talk with the students and faculty members. We also visited the Yong-Dong-Po Industrial Mission and learned more of the ongoing church sponsored community organizing in squatter communities.

The third leg of the trip was to Taiwan. We visited faculty colleagues, seminary students, and church leaders we knew from our years at Tainan Theological Seminary. It was gratifying to see how programs begun in the 1959 to 1963 period had blossomed under the leadership of students and church leaders with whom we had worked in our time there. The policy of shifting resources from supporting foreign missionaries to under-girding the work of local leaders was bearing fruit.

In 1998, we were surprised and pleased to have another invitation to visit South Korea, this time from Kim Dae-Jung when he was elected president of South Korea. We were part of a group of a dozen people from USA and European church communities invited to his inauguration. Kim was first elected to office in South Korea in 1963, but because of his political activities under the military government of President Park, he had suffered imprisonment and exile. He had long been a supporter of the church's work with university students, labor unions, and the urban poor. During one period of exile, he and his wife were provided a place by Union Theological Seminary in New York to study and work.

Upon return to Asia, he settled in Japan, and continued his work with those who sought democratic changes in the government of South Korea. He was kept under surveillance by South Korean intelligence agents and was kidnapped from a Tokyo hotel where he was attending a conference in 1973. A number of us worked to enlist the US government to use its resources to find out what had happened to him. The American CIA discovered that the Korean CIA had arrested him and learned that the kidnappers had planned to load him on a motor launch and cross the strait from Japan to Korea. There was good reason to believe they might dump him overboard on the way. With pressure from the U.S. ambassador, a military helicopter was dispatched to monitor the boat across the strait and the Japan Maritime Self-Defense Force pursued the kidnapper's vessel. Kim survived the transit and was imprisoned upon arrival.

During the Carter administration, while Kim was imprisoned and under a death sentence, pressure was brought to bear on the Korean government that if any harm came to him while in custody it would damage US relations with South Korea. Relationships with the United States were important to Korea, as they continue to be, and his sentence was commuted. Eventually, the political situation changed, when after the violent quelling of university students' protests, and the international backlash, the military government began to back off use of repressive force. Kim was released from prison and returned to politics. He was grateful for the support he received from the World Council of Churches and its member churches throughout the world through this period. For the 1998 WCC Assembly, Kim sent a letter that noted, "The WCC has stood with the church, intellectuals, students, and other people of Korea during their long years of struggle to achieve democracy and reunification. I will be forever thankful for the solidarity and support it extended to me all those years I was in agony."

He was successful in his fourth bid for the presidency in 1998. At the inauguration celebration, Kathy and I were received at the presidential residence by President Kim and his wife and received a plaque that noted our support for "the struggle for democracy in Korea over the past two decades." There was, at the same time, an International Urban Mission Seminar going on at the German founded Evangelical Academy in Korea to which I was invited to talk about the history and future of Urban and Industrial Mission.

Kim received the Nobel Peace Prize in 2000 for his work in the democratization of South Korea. He was also instrumental in bettering relationships with North Korea and providing opportunities for families to be reunited across the borders, known as the "Sunshine Policy." Throughout his career, he experienced much hardship and sacrifice, as he was arrested multiple times and there were five assassination attempts on his life. When he died of natural causes in 2009, Sam Kobia, then General Secretary of the World Council of Churches, noted, "Of Kim Dae-Jung it can truly be said, 'Blessed are the peacemakers, for they will be called the children of God.'"

In 2001, I received the Yale Divinity School "Distinction in Ministry" award. The commendation highlighted our work in the East Harlem Protestant Parish, the World Council of Churches, and particularly my role in engaging church participation in community organizing. It was on that occasion that I preached on the theme of "Exposure and Risk." Classmates and colleagues whom I esteem have also received this award in recent years – Bob Batchelder, Masao Takenaka, William F. May, and Gregor Thompson Goethals.

In thinking of the future, I penned some thoughts for Yale Divinity School at our 50th anniversary reunion about how the church will look in 50 years. These are included in the appendix, along with a fuller essay on *Exposure and Risk* which I wrote during my time with the World Council of Churches.

Kathy and I were also honored by the Presbyterian Health, Education, and Welfare Association with the John Park Lee Award in 2007. This is an award acknowledging a "ministry of justice and human welfare." We traveled to New Orleans for that presentation and saw firsthand the long-term devastation that Hurricane Katrina had wrought, a pulling back of the curtain on the racial and economic divides that still characterized this nation and their city.

Finally, our lives are increasingly enriched over time by our sons and their families. We still grieve over the disappearance of our son Sam at the end of 1983. At the time, he was in his final year at Yale Divinity School. He was planning to be ordained and had arranged an internship in a church after graduation. Sam was talented in sports and music, as well as in his academic and justice pursuits. Sam wrote some lively papers about liberation movements in Africa, the Mexican Revolution, and the Russian Revolution. He went to Zimbabwe, invited by our family friend and first democratically elected president, Canaan Banana, to teach in a school working with young people who had been in the liberation army and were coming back to high school.

Sam had many God-given gifts to serve the church. The mystery of his disappearance has never seen solved. We have resisted having any kind of memorial service that would signal we have completely given up hope that he might still be alive. We anticipate that we are going to meet him when we come around the great welcome table in the life to come. In 2004, marking the 20th anniversary of the graduation of his class, there was a celebration of his life at Yale Divinity School and a scholarship fund was created in Sam's name for Asian or African students who demonstrate a commitment to peace and justice ministries. Losing him is a constant reminder of how fragile life is and how important it is to treasure those we love.

Our first son, John, was born while we were in the East Harlem Protestant Parish. He is a talented musician and explored that as a vocation when he studied for a year at the University of Geneva conservatory. He decided music was not his career path and graduated from Hampshire College where met his future wife, Dorothy. After graduation they both studied law, he at Columbia and she at Rutgers. Upon graduation from law school they both had clerkships with Federal Court judges and then began their careers in corporate law firms. After a time, they decided that they wanted to live and work in a place where they could give priority to their family and involve themselves in the life of a community, rather than pursuing a career in a demanding urban corporate law practice. They moved to Northampton, near Hampshire, the college they loved. John found work as legal counsel for an insurance company and Dorothy concentrated on family and community activities. They have three wonderful children - Hannah Grace, Abraham Milton, and Eli Daniel.

When John was courting Dorothy, he told her he wanted to raise their children "religious," as he had been. She came from a Jewish family that was not particularly religious, but which embraced their Jewish identity. John converted to Judaism and their family is active in a lively synagogue. We enjoy celebrating the Passover Seder with Dorothy's extended family and the beauty of the Hebrew prayers and ceremony.

Our son Peter, the next eldest, now lives at Stony Point, a conference center connected to the Presbyterian Church, an hour from New York City. He has battled mental illness almost his entire adult life, with the onset of schizophrenia beginning in college. Although he went through periods of hospitalization initially, with the help of interested and competent psychiatrists and good therapeutic programs, Peter has become increasingly self-reliant. We are grateful that he has made a good home for himself and found a supportive community at the Stony Point Center as well as generous support from the mental health programs of Rockland County. We visit Peter often. He is a thoughtful and reflective man, who has a poetic soul and a gift for making lasting friendships. His love is a great strength for us.

Our youngest son, Adam, was born in Taiwan and came to the United States when he was one year old. After attending elementary school in New York City and Montclair, NJ, he went to the International School in Geneva and then to Brown University, where he met his future wife, Cynthia. He is also a musician and played with jazz combos in college and while he was attending law school at Rutgers. While Cynthia pursued doctoral studies in English at NYU Adam worked with the Legal Services Administration, which serves people who cannot afford to hire lawyers, but who need legal assistance to see their way through the court system.

After getting her doctorate, Cynthia was offered a teaching position at Wittenberg College in Ohio to which she and Adam moved. She is a recognized expert in feminist literature. Her dissertation studied the influence of women readers on literature published in the 18th century. Adam took a teaching position at Northern Kentucky University's Salmon P. Chase School of Law. In his 13 years there, he gained a reputation for his work in developing programs of support for African American students and students with Appalachian roots who were the first in their families to pursue higher education. He then taught for three years at the University of Baltimore Law School, followed by a year at Southern Methodist University in Dallas, commuting from Springfield, OH. He now teaches at the University of Dayton Law School, only half an hour from home.

They have two children. The older, Lilith, was named by her mother in honor of the mythical figure who, in legends around the Garden of Eden story, was created as Adam's female companion. Lilith left him when he insisted that she be subservient to him. Their son, Samuel, is named for Kathy's father and our son Sam.

Adam and Cynthia, along with their children, spent a semester as Fulbright scholars in the Czech Republic a few years ago. We were proud that those with whom they worked said to Adam and Cynthia as they were departing, "You're the first Americans who have come not to tell us what to do, but to learn from us what we think."

Having had the opportunity in writing this memoir to look back over the 20th century decades of my own efforts and experiences in the ministry and mission of the Christian church, I am deeply grateful for all the blessings God has given us in this moment of history - family, friends, interesting places to call home, and challenging work.

As I end these reflections, I must confess that I cannot remember living through a more troubling period in our public life. On my 80th birthday in 2005, I wrote a letter to my family from which I want to quote because it still expresses what I still believe to be true.

> To have national leadership with no scruples about telling lies and grossly manipulating the public, to be engaging us in disastrous wars and violating basic principles of what has made us proud to be Americans makes it painful to read the morning newspaper and watch the evening news on TV. It helps that Kathy and I do this together and that we have a family of children and grandchildren, other relatives and friends who share our outrage, but at this point it is very difficult to see what lies ahead. We keep looking for national leadership but cannot see it. Instead we see the growing gap between rich and poor, the deterioration of public life and those who are losing their homes, growing unemployment, and the shameful condition of the U.S, pharmaceutical and health delivery systems.

Underlying all of these is the continuing power of corporations and the wealthy in controlling politicians and government policy. Where is commitment to the common good and evidence of love and respect underlying our public life? A current op-ed column in the New York Times underlines the limitations of a constitutional system which gives the rights of persons to corporations and parodies the Declaration of Independence and popular songs by substituting "corporations" for "people": "Of the corporations, by the corporations and for the corporations. We the corporations. Corporations that need corporations are the luckiest corporations in the world. Power to the corporations!"

While Trey and I worked together to produce this text and rehearsed my experiences, I came to realize that at many moments I was indeed encountering throughout the USA and all over the world the many places where Tillich's vision of the autonomous spirit of God is at work in inspiring human beings, created in God's image, to join the glorious company of prophets, saints and martyrs. That "Great Coming Church" is already visible. Some of those who are building it are mentioned in this story we have told. I decided that "The Great Coming Church" should be added to the title for much of what was in the vision of the Student Christian movement and the ecumenical movement mentioned at the beginning of this effort can be seen blossoming across the earth. My own conviction that the powerful inflowing of the resurrection generating new life comes exactly in obedience to Christ's call to take up the cross and follow him to the places where hunger, poverty, injustice and despair seem to rule – and through our willingness to undertake the call to exposure and risk.

Our inspiration now has to rise from the bright and coming generation. We pray for health and power for them to use their lives to fulfill the real possibilities which exist to redeem our nation and make a world where all people can realize their full human possibilities.

It is my belief, and also my experience and understanding that in our Lord Jesus Christ, God has given us a pattern that, when we are prepared to act in ways that may risk our security, beliefs, affirmations and ideologies, we are offered assurance that these actions will be successful. It is in these moments that we are offered the good news of resurrection, new life, new possibilities, and fresh ways of realizing the fulfillment of God's intention for creation.

When beginning this memoir, the working the title was "Exposure and Risk," but also considered "The Great Coming Church." Neither title seems wholly appropriate, but I am committed to keeping them. I am convinced that God is working to bring into being during the coming decades a church that will witness to God's presence and it will surprise us in relation to its shape and relevance to what is happening in the world.

# APPENDIX 1

— ✌ —

# Exposure and Risk

by Rev. George Todd

THIS ADDRESS WAS *given to the Yale Divinity School Class of 1951, at its 50*[th] *reunion, in 2001.*

**World-affirming Mission** – Christians are called to be involved in all spheres of the life of the world. The watchwords are "Christian presence," "a listening ministry," "incarnational mission," "dialogue," and "letting the world set the agenda." The testimony that God is sovereign; that Jesus Christ is now Lord over all creation and all of history; and that Christ is present and active in all events and in all of life is the basis of these ministries.

One witnesses to the faith and communicates it by the seriousness with which a Christian takes the world and its structures. If God is present in the shop, the factory, the government office, the school, the community organization, Christians must go there to meet God. They must look and listen and find out what God is doing there. They affirm that God has a purpose for each person in his or her daily callings within the structures of society.

It is the mission of the church to affirm God's presence in all realms of life, to seek to discern God's action there, and to seek obedience to God's will through the action of Christians in the world. It is the mission of the church to bring each person to an awareness of God's call to obedience in the use of the skills and the exercise of responsibility in whatever place each may be set. The work situation is an arena for Christian obedience.

Biblical passages which assert the Lordship of Christ over principalities and powers: (Colossians 1:16-17 In *Him all things in heaven and on earth*

137

*were created, things visible and invisible, whether thrones or dominions or rulers or powers – all things have been created through Him and for Him. He Himself is before all things, and in Him all things hold together.)* and passages underlining secular occupation as "ordained of God"). Rom. 13:1. *Let every person be subject to the governing authorities; for there is no authority except from God and those authorities that exist have* been instituted by God.) and (1 Corinthians 7: 17, 24: *Let each of you lead the life that the Lord has assigned you. In whatever condition you are called, brothers and sisters, there remain with God.)* are relevant texts.

The message that God became a human being, and participated in human history, means for those "missionaries" that the arena of human life and work is hallowed by God because God participates in it. God is present and acting there. We witness to God's presence by responding to this active presence already there.

**Prophetic and Eschatological Mission.** Many social action ministries concerned with planning and building better cities, reforming economic systems, working with issues such as housing, racial justice, environment, and quality of life are motivated by the biblical imperatives against injustice and lovelessness and by the biblical vision of a Heavenly City in which Shalom is fulfilled. God's intentions for his people are revealed through God's relationship with the people of Israel, in the law and the covenant.

What we are meant to be is made visible in Jesus Christ. The impossible possibilities are held before us in the Sermon on the Mount. The eschatological promise of what we are to become, detailed in the scriptures, and constantly being revealed in surprising signs of the power and principalities of love to be revealed in God's time, give urgency to act in this present urban and industrial society under the power of those promises. Mission is performed by calling people to use their human capacity to dream dreams and see visions of the possibilities in human life.

The Bible and the experience of the Christian community give to the church the aims, goals, norms, and value with which to judge the metropolis and to inspire it with visions of what God wants the city to be. The focus of the church on basic moral and spiritual values witnesses to the power of Christ to free people from technological and economic determinism. These mission programs call persons to make choices in favor of values to which they become consciously committed as they build cities. Christians must also pronounce a strong "no" against sinful and demonic structures and Christians must act for change.

One weakness of action of this type is that the work of identifying evil and defining the good can sometimes be so absorbing that Christians are diverted from the direct action needed to bring about changes now. In the midst of crisis, the confusion of continual change, and the facing of massive, intractable problems, this style of ministry offers guidelines and hope through bringing more clearly into view the possibilities which God has given to his people to use their skill. This kind of work helps people in their capacity to create and provides the basis on which to respond to the prophet's "no" to the dehumanizing features of urban and economic life.

**Mission as "cross-bearing"** – Alongside (and sometime over against) those with world-affirming or with prophetic mission styles stand those whose understanding of mission begin with the cross. For them, the other two styles must be continually tested by the experience of this third approach. They say that God is calling the church to be present at the places where suffering, pains, oppression, and bondage are most keenly felt. There is a kind of Christ-mysticism which takes with literal seriousness that if Christ is to be met anywhere now, Christ is to be found with the poor. If one wants to know and meet Christ, one must go where Christ is. Mission is fulfilled through sharing the life of the poor and joining in the struggle of the poor for liberation, in the name of Christ.

The church witnesses as it takes upon itself the sin and suffering of the metropolis, bearing in its own body the pain of society. As the church is present and takes form at the points where people are suffering, where brokenness, alienation, sickness, despair, poverty, and death prevail, the crucified and resurrected Lord is made known through his church in healing, reconciling, and health-giving action. As Christians "take up the cross" they meet Christ and may also become mediators of Christ to their fellows. In many parts of the world comes the testimony of Christians who have chosen to work as unskilled laborers in industry, or to live in squatter shacks or slum tenements, or who have joined the organized efforts of workers or peasants, or rural poor protesting oppression and claiming a just share of the world's goods. They believe that the church should be poor, should be with the poor, and should serve the poor.

The story of Christ's own life and passion, and texts such as Luke 4:18-19, The *Spirit of the Lord is upon me, because he has anointed me to bring good news to the poor. He has sent me to proclaim release to the captives and recovery of sight to the blind, to let the oppressed go free, to proclaim the year of the Lord's favor;* Matthew 16:24-5, *If anyone wants to become my followers, let them deny themselves and take up their cross and follow me, for those who want to save their life will lose it and those who lose their life for my sake will find it;* along with Exodus 3:7-8, *I have observed the misery of my people. I have heard their cry. I have come down to deliver them, and to bring them to a good and broad land, a land flowing with milk and honey;* Luke 1: 47-55, *My soul magnifies the Lord and my spirit rejoices in God my Savior for he has looked with favor on the lowliness of his servant...he has shown strength with his arm; he has scattered the proud in the thoughts of their hearts; he has brought down the powerful from their thrones and lifted up the lowly; he has filled the hungry with good things and sent the rich away empty;* Matthew 25:34-46, *I was hungry and you gave me food, I was thirsty and you gave me something to drink, I was a stranger and you welcomed me, I was naked and you gave me clothing, I was sick and you took care of me, I was in prison and you visited me...just as you did it to one of the least of these you did it to me;* speak to such missioners about the shape their mission should take. Christ's resurrection promise is to be experienced and known at the point where life is risked in being present with and for those who suffer.

# APPENDIX 2

## Some Thoughts About How (Might) (Will) (Should) the Church Look in 2050

### Rev. George Todd

*EACH YEAR SINCE 1952, a group of Yale Divinity School graduates has corresponded. As a part of that exercise, we assigned ourselves a topic about which we shared experience, ideas, and reflections. I wrote this as my contribution to that exchange in the year 2000.*

In the late 1930s, Paul Tillich predicted the end of the Protestant era. He told us that the Reformation had run its course and that by the end of the 20th century the historic Protestant denominations, though still very much in existence, would have become like museums, preserved by people who had a nostalgia for traditional music, liturgy and architecture, but no longer living vehicles of the Spirit. He called us to look for the ways the Spirit of God could be discerned in "autonomous realms" bringing into being new forms and shapes for the communities and institutions emerging as bearers of the Spirit and power of the Gospel in the world and in history.

In the 1960s and 1970s some of us thought there might be some signs that this was happening. The World Student Christian Federation, in its *Life and Mission of the Church* studies in the 1950s, and the World Council of Churches in its *Missionary Structures of the Congregation* study in the '60s and '70s challenged what they described as "morphological fundamentalism." By this they meant the idolatry of the received forms of congregational and denominational ways of being the church.

There was a period in the '60s and '70s of vigorous experimentation. The Iona Community, Taizé, industrial missions in England and the USA, Gossner Mission in Germany, Evangelical Academies in Germany, French Worker Priests, Metropolitan Associates of Philadelphia, East Harlem Protestant Parish and its related parishes in New Haven, Chicago, Cleveland and Denver and many more flowered in this period. There emerged a number of Ecumenical and Urban Training Centers developing new forms of formation for ministry. Revolts in the city fostered the emergence of local and national racial and ethnic coalitions of Christians inventing new forms of being the church as they sought power for their constituencies.

Following World War II dozens of countries under colonial rule achieved independence. With them, "missions" in those countries initiated by American and European missionary agencies, became self-governing, independent churches. In the '50s they joined the World Council of Churches as peers with the churches that had earlier spawned and governed them. Many of these new national churches, as well as new national and regional Councils of Churches in Africa, Asia and Latin America were blossoming in ways that looked quite different from the ones missionaries came from.

In some 40 cities in the United States, ecumenical or interfaith instrumentalities had come into being through which churches in major metropolitan areas responded to the revolts and to the critical urban justice issues such as housing, employment, education and health care. By the early '70s a number of new national bodies had appeared, quite different in shape and agenda from the traditional church bodies from which they sprang and which gave them auspice - Bread for the World, Interfaith Center for Corporate Responsibility, the Inter-religious Foundation for Community Organization, and Impact (a Washington-based center with chapters in many states for church monitoring of local and state governance).

This ferment seemed to be pointing to a time, by the end of the millennium, for the appearance of the new kind of church that Tillich was foretelling. This was not to be. By the mid-1970s institutional backlash was setting in. Much of the above activity was drastically curtailed or disappeared altogether. The denominations gave themselves to perennial institutional reorganization, often based on business management models. Ethnic initiatives and ministries, although successful in gaining visibility and important places in the staffs and decision-making posts in many of the historic denominations, soft-pedaled justice agendas in favor of work to build and maintain ethnic congregations, mostly on traditional models. The efforts of COCU (Commission on Church Union) to engineer church union among major Protestant bodies endlessly focused its energies on finding bureaucratic and creedal ways of bringing into being the oneness they sought. (They finally have settled on jettisoning that agenda in favor of encouraging the partners to find ways of collaborating in efforts of social witness, education and evangelism without waiting for a single structural solution).

Councils of Churches, whether they are city, state or national, *should* be the arenas where the traditional churches should come to understand one another's priorities, programs and convictions. They should be arenas where churches could discover ways to collaborate at points where their separate programs and priorities coincide. Instead, Councils of Churches typically work with a small group of "representatives" that develop the Council's own programs which the churches are asked to support alongside their own priorities and programs. In the last decade most of the denominations have also been absorbed in issues of gender politics concerning ordination of women and maintaining sexuality tests for ordination of clergy and church officers.

As we enter the 21st century it may be that Tillich's predictions are coming true as seen in what has been going on (and not going on) in the denominations over the past 25 years. Certainly the decline in membership of most of the "mainline churches" would seem to point that way. Most of them, through their endowments, have sustained their fiscal viability and could surely be with us through this century.

Having looked backward, let me now look ahead. I have evoked the 1960s because I believe strongly that we experienced there a foretaste of many of the new shapes the church will have to take in the coming decades. It mystifies me that for the most part the history of the churches in that period remains mostly a blank in written materials and in seminary curriculum. Much of what *is* taught and reported is misleading. So first of all my hope is that there will be an appropriation of much of the experience and literature of that period as people work to make the church effective and relevant.

Here are several predictions I make:

## The Congregation

The congregation will continue to be vital in a world increasingly global with many forces continuing to pull people in many directions. The existence of many continuing relatively small communities of people bound by common faith who know each other across generations, across ethnic, economic and professional lines, will be valued and cherished. There the Gospel will be spoken, taught, celebrated and passed on from generation to generation. Affirmation of God's grace and the calling into faithfulness through rites of baptism, confirmation, marriage and funerals will continue to be cherished. Threats of de-personalization will be powerfully resisted through these affirmations of the importance of the value of each individual life in God's sight and in the context of community. Frequent Eucharist and celebrations of the holy festivals will continue to witness before the world and to the congregation itself the existence of a community of saints which is global and joins us to the past and future.

I believe we will be seeing new kinds of congregations alongside those drawn from geographical parishes. Members may be drawn from vocational groups, sectors of city life such as health care, politics, education, commerce, industry and communications. We will see the continuous emergence of intentional groups committed to exploring the will of God for their daily work or committed to work together on issues such as poverty and peace. Congregations will no longer be nearly as centered around the role of a single or small group of clergy persons. There will be much greater access to contemporary Biblical and theological scholarship

144

for laypersons. There will be serious reflection and emergence of new ways of understanding ordination. There will be much fuller recognition of the variety of ministries and callings under God, with congregational affirmations, support and expectations for every member to explore, as Christian vocation, the occupations in which they find themselves.

### New Structures of Collaboration

We cannot envision what these will look like, but most congregations will recognize the necessity of collaborating with other congregations in fulfilling their ministry in their neighborhood, their region and in the nation. This will be especially true for addressing major social issues, witnessing to God's judgment against corruption and injustice and working to heal and to create just governing structures. More often than not local Councils of Churches are functioning very inadequately in these respects. New coalitions such as those represented by Habitat for Humanity and Bread for the World will be coming into being. Such ecumenical and interfaith structures will be emerging. Churches will be moving toward collaborative work through these structures as a common expression of faith and witness by mid-century. It will also be important so that congregations in particular locations can be linked not only nationally but to churches in other parts of the world. The Interfaith Center for Corporate Responsibility is a model of showing how several hundred church bodies and congregations can explore how to direct their assets toward investments which support economic development, protect the environment and have fair employment practices.

### The Ecumenical Movement

We will see radical changes in the ways that Christian faith communities relate to one another. I believe we are seeing now the phasing out of traditional "councils of churches," locally, nationally and internationally, in the ways they now function. Christians will be discovering one another across confessional lines and working together to witness to their faith and in finding ways to respond to the needs of the world through exploration of a variety of new institutional forms. I'm glad that COCU has shelved its search for structural union. Among official leaders of the church there is not nearly enough recognition that hundreds of such alliances are already going on in all parts of our country and in the world. It is hard to see clearly what this will look like in the years ahead but it is happening.

We will have come, along with continuing tensions and antagonisms among fundamentalists of various world religions, into a period of *very rich relationships and encounters among people of various historic faith groups.* Christian theologians will be giving major attention to the ways in which Biblical theology affirms God's sovereignty, presence and activities through other faith traditions. They will be spelling out ways that our Biblical faith may be understood to *mandate* taking other faith traditions seriously, with the expectation of encountering God's presence and the revelation of God's intentions for creation through those traditions.

### Empowerment

There will be a sharper sense within the churches of the scandal and apostasy of the gap between the rich and poor among nations and within nations. This will be particularly on the conscience of the churches in Europe and North America. Autonomous national churches and national and regional Councils in developing countries and regions have become much more articulate and able to make their voices heard across national and regional lines within the global Christian community. There will be a much wider understanding than there is now for the need of Christians to support efforts of justice and equity. There will be increased sensitivity and understanding that charity and development are not sufficient without attention to changing unjust political and economic structures.

In the years ahead, the question of *power* and *participation* will emerge in a more central way in theology and in defining the mission of the church and its ministry. The implications of this will become increasingly evident in the life of congregations and denominations as well as in national, regional and global religious institutions.

Since the mid-1960s and increasingly now our church's fullest acquiring and use of political power has been through the participation of the church in neighborhood and metropolitan community organizing. Across the country in virtually every metropolitan center, organizations created through the initiative of congregations have brought into being coalitions of typically 30-60 congregations, synagogues, and mosques building power bases through which their members who are residents can define agendas of their concerns and through their combined numbers achieve power to affect change. This phenomenon is still not widely recognized and understood among our churches, in our seminaries, or among national church leaders. This is a growing movement with an increasing number of professional organizers who are trained both in theology and organizing skills.

Such congregations are playing a significant role in accomplishing a major change in American society and effecting reforms in the way our country is governed. These organizations are, in many communities, effectively addressing the functioning of American democracy. They are opening up new possibilities for ordinary citizens and for many of the most disadvantaged groups in society to have access to participation in the decision-making processes of American cities and states. There is a growing academic literature describing this phenomenon and envisioning the future possibilities I point to here. This is happening although there is little recognition or affirmation of it by current leaders of our church's national structures.

Church-based para-political organizations in Asia are discovering this work as a form of service toward building functional democratic societies that, in our time, parallels the contribution of mission-founded and church-sponsored schools, hospitals and social service agencies in the past century.

I envy you readers who are, and will be, participating in carrying forward such changes as these.

# Bibliography

*15 years of CO: reports of the ACPO Assessment meeting, Kathmandu, Nepal, April 16-21, 1986.* Kowloon, Hong Kong: ACPO, 1987.

Alinsky, Saul David. *Reveille for Radicals.* Chicago: University of Chicago Press, 1946.

Bonhoeffer, Dietrich. *Life Together.* 1st Ed. New York: Harper & Row, 1954.

Bonhoeffer, Dietrich. *The Cost of Discipleship.* 2nd Ed. Ed. New York: Macmillan, 1959.

Cox, Harvey Gallagher. *The Secular City.* London: S.C.M. Press, 1966.

*Documents on the Struggle for Democracy in Korea.* Tokyo: Shinkyo Shuppansha, 1975.

Ellul, Jacques. *The Meaning of the City.* Grand Rapids, MI.: Eerdmans, 1970.

Ellul, Jacques. *The Presence of the Kingdom.* Philadelphia: Westminster Press, 1951.

Goodman, Grace Ann. *Rocking the Ark; Nine Case Studies of Traditional Churches in Process of Change.* New York: Division of Evangelism, United Presbyterian Church in the U.S.A., 1968.

Green, Clifford J. *Churches, Cities, and Human Community: Urban Ministry in the United States, 1945-1985.* Grand Rapids, Mich.: W.B. Eerdmans, 1996.

Green, R.H. *Transnational Corporations: a Challenge for Churches and Christians.* Geneva: World Council of Churches, 1982.

Kim, Yong. *Messiah and Minjung: Christ's solidarity with the people for new life*. Kowloon, Hong Kong: Christian Conference of Asia. Urban Rural Mission, 1992.

Kobia, Samuel. *The Quest for Democracy in Africa*. Nairobi: National Council of Churches of Kenya, 1993.

Lewin, Hugh. *A Community of Clowns: Testimonies of People in Urban Rural Mission*. Geneva: WCC Publications, 1987.

Maglaya, Felipe E. *Organizing people for power: a manual for organizers*. 2nd ed. Tokyo: Asian Committee for People's Organization, 1978.

Miller, Mike. *A Community Organizer's Tale: People and Power in San Francisco*. Berkeley: Heyday Books, 2009.

Miller, Mike. *Community Organizing: a Brief Introduction*. Milwaukee: Euclid Avenue Press, 2012.

Tillich, Paul, and James Luther Adams. *The Protestant Era*. Chicago: University of Chicago Press, 1948.

*The Church for Others and the Church for the World: a Quest for Structures for Missionary Congregations*. Geneva: World Council of Churches, 1968.

*Transnational Corporations: a Challenge for Churches and Christians*. Geneva, Switzerland: Commission on the Churches' Participation in Development, World Council of Churches, 1982.

Wickham, E. R. *Church and People in an Industrial City*. London: Lutterworth Press, 1957.

Younger, George D. *From New Creation to Urban Crisis: A History of Action Training Ministries, 1962-1975*. Chicago: Center for the Scientific Study of Religion, 1987.

*World Council of Churches Urban Industrial Mission Publications\**

Hargleroad, Bobbi Wells. *Struggle to be Human: Stories of Urban-Industrial Mission*. Geneva: Urban and Industrial Mission Desk, Commission on World Mission and Evangelism, World Council of Churches, 1974.

Howell, Leon. *People are the Subject: Stories of Urban Rural Mission*. Geneva: World Council of Churches. Commission on World Mission and Evangelism, 1980.

*Mission and Justice: Urban and Industrial Mission at Work*. Geneva: World Council of Churches, 1977.

\*Some of these publications are currently out of print. However, many of these publications can be found at various theological institutions such as Union Theological Seminary in the city of New York or Yale Divinity School in New Haven, Ct. Likewise, some of these publications or other useful resources are available by visiting and contacting the World Council of Churches at http://www.oikoumene.org.

Made in the USA
San Bernardino, CA
26 May 2016